Mariah Balaban AND Jennifer Shields

STUDY AWAY

Mariah Balaban is a 25-year-old freelance writer and enthusiastic traveler. In high school she participated in educational programs in Alsace-Lorraine, Oxford, and the West Indies. She earned her bachelor's degree at Sarah Lawrence College, and spent her senior year in Paris. She currently lives in New York City and is working on a screenplay and a guidebook to Amsterdam.

Jennifer Shields, a native New Yorker, is a recent graduate of the University of St. Andrews in Scotland, where she earned a joint master's degree in Russian and Economics. She has spent two summers in Russia at Moscow State University attending an intensive Russian language program and is continuing her studies at the European University in St. Petersburg. Although Jennifer ended up finding the college of her dreams in St. Andrews, she went through a lot of difficulty searching for it. The process made her aware of the need for this book.

STUDY AWAY

STUDY AWAY

The Unauthorized Guide to College Abroad

Mariah Balaban
AND Jennifer Shields

ANCHOR BOOKS

A Division of Random House, Inc.

New York

AN ANCHOR BOOKS ORIGINAL, OCTOBER 2003

Copyright © 2003 by Mariah Balaban and Jennifer Shields

All rights reserved under International and Pan-American
Copyright Conventions.
Published in the United States by Anchor Books, a division of
Random House, Inc., New York, and simultaneously in Canada by
Random House of Canada Limited, Toronto.

Anchor Books and colophon are registered trademarks of Random
House, Inc.

Library of Congress Cataloging-in-Publication Data
Shields, Jennifer, 1980–
Study away : the unauthorized guide to college abroad /
Jennifer Shields and Mariah Balaban.
p.   cm.
ISBN 1-4000-3189-3 (pbk.)
1. Foreign study—Handbooks, manuals, etc.   2. American
students—Foreign countries—Handbooks, manuals, etc.
I. Balaban, Mariah, 1977–   II. Title.
LB2376.S45 2003
370.116—dc21
2003052172

Photo permissions can be found at the end of the book.

Book design by Mia Risberg

www.anchorbooks.com

Printed in the United States of America
10 9 8 7 6 5 4 3 2 1

*To our parents
who gave us the support we needed
to pursue our own adventures abroad.*

ACKNOWLEDGMENTS

We would like to thank the following people, without whose help this book would not have been possible (or would have at least been a whole lot more difficult): Eric Adolfsen, Shaw Bowman, Julie Doughty, Laura Flam, Eric Iversen, Victoria Joffe, Tom McCabe, Marjorie Nieuwenhuis, Daniel Rudder, Alexandra Shelley, Boni Grossman Smith, and Amanda Urban.

CONTENTS

STUDY AWAY

Welcome to

STUDY AWAY

———

This book was written by and for people like yourself. How do we know what you're like? Well, the very fact that you're reading this introduction proves that you're curious, the sort of person who might seek out new and challenging experiences. It also means that you're looking for information about colleges off the beaten path, and that's exactly what you'll find here.

Study Away will tell you the whats, whys, wheres, and hows of going to college outside of the United States—whether you're looking to get your degree abroad or just to visit for a semester or two. This book was independently written. We are not affiliated with any larger interest; we have not been paid by anyone to say nice things about universities. We haven't sold any ad space, we've written this book solely for students, and we've tried to be as objective as possible.

You may be wondering why we have written such a book. It was Jenny's idea. After making the decision to leave the States to pursue her university education, she was frustrated to discover that there was a serious lack of college guidebooks on universities in other countries. Since she was lucky enough to know a little bit about where she wanted to go, it was easier for her to look (mainly on-line) for information. But what about the students who aren't even aware of what their options are?

This book will show you the many colleges and universities outside of the U.S. that teach entirely in English, many of which follow a liberal arts curriculum and offer American degrees. There are also lots of universities in English-speaking countries that welcome American and other international students. We've highlighted the best of these universities, ones that are well established and generally much cheaper than their American counterparts. We found them through exhaustive on-line searches, by poring through hundreds of web sites and catalogs, interviewing students and administrators, and even attending a conference for study abroad counselors.

We've done all the legwork so you don't have to. All you have to do is go to the bookstore and pick up a copy of our book. Call us trailblazers if you want to (although that seems a bit dramatic), or better yet, read our book and be one yourself.

Happy hunting!

—Mariah Balaban
and Jennifer Shields

WHY STUDY ABROAD?

In a survey sent out to students, we posed the question, "What was your favorite aspect of going abroad?" One girl responded, "Living in Madrid, I discovered a home that was not introduced to me by my heritage, my parents, or my birth. It was solely mine. I believe that these experiences truly reflect who I am."

To us, the most important aspect of living in another country is the sense of independence that it allows you. Far from home and way past the boundaries of familiarity, you can grow in ways you may have never thought possible. As one alumnus of United States International University in Nairobi put it, "The greatest benefit of multicultural exposure is the confidence one gets to mix freely with people without shying away. It helped me to start a bank at only twenty-five."

So whether you've always dreamed of packing up and shipping out, or are even just the least bit curious about studying abroad, you should consider the following benefits of going to college in another country:

You'll learn more.

No matter what subject you're looking to get your degree in, you can benefit invaluably from an international education. Having the opportunity to live and study with students and professors from all around the world allows you to gain a truly global perspective and understanding. This is important on a personal level, but will also be very impressive to future employers or graduate schools. Another advantage to studying abroad is that the world will be your textbook. When Mariah went to Paris for part of her junior year, she took a class on the history of political power in France as seen through its capital's monuments. Reading novels and eyewitness accounts combined with walking tours and field trips allowed her to gain a much more profound understanding of the subject. When what you're learning is no longer centuries away, or in some far-off land, but immediately tangible, it allows you to really connect with your education.

It's cheaper.

Generally speaking, universities outside the States give you more for your money. Not only is tuition lower overseas, but many undergraduate degree programs last for only three years, and often offer merit- and need-based scholarships to international students. Also, if a college is accredited in the States, you can apply for the same types of federal aid packages and scholarships that you would be eligible to use if you were studying in the U.S. Some good web sites to check out for more information on funding your education are:

www.fafsa.ed.gov
www.finaid.org
www.college-scholarships.com
www.internationalstudentloans.com

You just might avoid the "college craze."

All you high school juniors and seniors out there are probably well aware of the phenomenon that journalists have dubbed the "college craze." The sleepless nights spent worrying about the SATs, the horror of trying to sum up your life's aspirations in two pages—we remember only too well how applying to college can feel like trying to get the last lifeboat off the *Titanic*. So for a smart and accomplished person like yourself, why is it so insanely competitive? Let's look at some facts:

In 1998, 2,468,600 people took the SAT I. Just three years later in 2001, that number rose to 2,850,000. By the year 2015, the number of Americans enrolling in colleges and universities is expected to increase by around 1.6 million, and as American schools increase their international recruiting policies, high school students from all over the world are competing for the same limited resources. The result is serious overcrowding. In 2001, Dartmouth College accepted so many of its applicants that 60 students were left homeless. The solution? $5,000 worth of free housing was offered to any student willing to defer for a year. This is not a problem unique to small liberal arts schools. In 2001, the University of Southern California received 3,000 more applicants than it had received the year before. To deal with its lack of housing, USC placed students in less than ideal conditions, lodging them in hotels and nearby frat houses.

Although the college-age population is booming, there are certainly enough colleges to go around, so why are some schools so crowded? If a school is harder to get into, does it mean that it's better? Not necessarily. Let's look at Muhlenberg College in Allentown, Pennsylvania, as an example. Since 1995, this small school has seen a 50% increase in its applications, due largely to a beefed-up marketing campaign. This allowed Muhlenberg to turn away over 60% of its applicants (up from only 25% in 1995), while maintaining the same freshman class size. According to Adam Rogers's article "Games Colleges Play" from *Newsweek*'s 2002 "How to Get into College" special edition, a high volume of applications, low acceptance rates, and high yields (the percentage of those accepted who actually enroll) "are the trifecta of college sex appeal." They contribute heavily to the way that student selectivity is calculated, and selectivity is the way that colleges are measured in the marketplace.

Another important "enrollment management" technique that colleges employ is Early Decision (or ED). Applying ED to a school basically means that you apply earlier than the other applicants, and if you get in, you must attend. Most universities with binding ED programs select a large percentage of the freshman class from ED applicants, leaving students from the regular applicant pool to compete for the remaining places. In his *Atlantic Monthly* article "The Early Decision Racket," journalist James Fallows wrote about a 1998 College Board meeting that discussed the effects of the Early Decision process: "All of them realized that binding ED programs allowed schools to feign a level of selectivity they don't really have."

So if selectivity is the unit by which colleges are measured, let's take a look at the instrument that measures them, the college ranking lists. The *U.S. News and World Report*'s "College Issue" is probably the most well-known college ranking list, and has an enormous following. (Its 2001 edition sold 40% more copies than the magazine's regular issues.) A recent study by Cornell professors Ronald G. Ehrenberg and James Monks found that changes in a school's *U.S. News and World Report* ranking can affect that school's admission statistics. Although they can seem like the be-all and end-all, these rankings should be taken with a grain of salt. Last year, for example, The California Institute of Technology rose from fourth to first in its ranking, due largely to the change in the way that *U.S. News and World Report* calculated school spending per student. Writes Ehrenberg, "Institutes don't change in quality from year to year—that's just *U.S. News* changing its formula."

These rankings have little to say about the real value of a particular education, because true quality is entirely judged by the person who finds it. As James Fallows points out, "CalTech, for example, is so different from Yale that whether it is better or worse depends on an individual student's aims." Of course, there are "name and network payoffs" from attending certain top schools, but Fallows writes, "The positive effects of these networks are certainly far less than the negative effects of not attending the University of Tokyo in Japan, or one of the *grande écoles* in France."

Going to college in another country allows you to bypass the U.S. admissions insanity and take advantage of all the opportunities that its locale might afford—imagine the benefits of being able to study marine biology in New Zealand, or art history in Rome.

And last but not least . . .

Sometimes, something's being very different from anything you know is a good enough reason to try it. Why not apply somewhere and see what happens?

CHOOSING AN
INTERNATIONAL UNIVERSITY

Now that you're acquainted with some of the advantages of studying abroad, you're going to need some pointers on choosing the type of international university that's right for you. Here are some questions that you'll probably want to ask:

What are the academics like?

Most of the universities listed in our book fall into a category known as "American overseas universities." Like many colleges in the States, these schools are built around a liberal arts framework, allowing you to choose your major after studying a somewhat broad curriculum for a year. Often, however, if you want to apply to a college that operates outside of the American system, you have to do a lot more thinking about what you want to study right off the bat. For example, when applying to U.K. universities, you must apply directly to a course or program of study, so not only do you have to know what you want to major in, you also need to hold the appropriate credentials. Does this mean that you have to know exactly what you want to do with your life right after high school? Not necessarily. We asked a British student about this, and she told us that in the U.K., "You just get used to it being a bit rigid, and most students just wing it." On the plus side, applying outside of the U.S. system can be very rewarding, since it allows you to dive right into your field of interest, and you can often graduate in only three years.

Marjorie Nieuwenhuis, Director of College Counseling at the United Nations International School (UNIS) and author of *A Parent's Guide to College Admissions,* has been sending her students to universities around the world for some 14 years. One word of advice she had for American students looking to leave the States was to keep in mind that "in terms of spreading your wings and doing a million different things that you have the luxury of doing in a liberal arts program, you just don't do that in a non-American university."

Is it accredited?

Simply put, if a university or college is accredited, its academic credits are recognized by a governing body. For American universities, here and abroad, there are a few standard accrediting organizations, like the Commission on Higher Education of the Middle States Association of Colleges and Schools, or the Accrediting Council for Independent Colleges and Schools. The issue of accreditation will probably only come up if you need to transfer your credits to another university, apply for grad school, or if an employer needs to verify that your college degree is legitimate.

But just because a university doesn't have American accreditation does not mean that its degree won't be recognized. Outside of America, universities are usually under the governance of their countries' ministries of education. (But you should be aware that "proprietary colleges," a.k.a. for-profit institutions, may not be recognized by their countries' governments and their degrees may be looked askance upon.) So who's actually doing the looking? Most major universities in the States have a department in admissions set up to assess overseas credentials. There are also a number of private businesses that contract similar services, usually to large corporations looking at job applicants.

How independent are you?

Another difference between American and non-American universities is that the latter expect a very high level of academic autonomy. Even at larger American universities where huge lectures and TAs are the norm, there is still the understanding that the professor will be monitoring your progress. This is not necessarily the case for many non-American universities. Usually, attendance at lectures is entirely up to the discretion of the student, and sometimes classes are assessed only through a midterm and a final exam. This may sound like a dream come true, but in these situations, students who are not self-motivated (or are bad at cramming) will probably find themselves falling through the cracks.

Where is it located?

Oftentimes, in non-American universities, there is not as much emphasis on the social aspects of college, the vital thing that we here in the States call "college life." This is why the location factor becomes especially important. If you are in a very small town and there is nothing to do on campus, chances are you may become bored very quickly. Try to find out as much as you can about extracurricular activities and facilities. A university with a student union will usually have student societies and organized events like parties, DJ nights, and live music. Many student unions have their own web sites, so you can check out what's going on at the school before applying.

Something else to look at when thinking about location is the language issue. Although all of the schools in our book instruct in English, it is important to ask yourself how comfortable you will feel living in a country where you may not speak the language. On the other hand, many students at American universities in non-English-speaking countries report that they do not really get a chance to be immersed in the local language because they are surrounded by English in the dorms and classrooms. So if learning another language is important to you, you will probably want to choose a program that specifically emphasizes language study.

(Conveniently enough, there are quite a few profiled in this book.) It is also interesting to mention that the majority of American students pursuing their degrees in the non-European world are of international descent, studying in places where they have family or where they can rediscover their roots. If you have a support network of friends and family in a particular country, that might be a good place to start off your college search.

STAYING SAFE AND OTHER
IMPORTANT ADVICE

In this section we share with you things we've picked up from our years of traveling and study abroad, so pay close attention!

Don't bring American baggage, or "When in Rome . . ."

Be willing to try new things and experience the new culture that surrounds you. Remember that you're not in America anymore. One American student studying in Australia wrote to us, "During my first week I remember heading out for a cup of coffee at about 8:00 P.M. After walking around downtown for about an hour looking for a place that was open, I realized that I was no longer in a society that carried on 24 hours a day! There was no Wal-Mart and no Denny's to head to in the wee hours of the night while taking that all-important late-night study break." As Americans, we're used to a certain level of convenience and speediness that (thankfully) just does not exist in other parts of the world. So when you're sitting in a café in Paris waiting for an hour for your waiter to bring you the bill, don't get upset. What you might think of as bad service, the French call "joie de vivre."

Also remember that people all over the world have different customs and act differently. This may seem like a no-brainer, but the subtleties of it can get you in trouble. Americans are remarkably casual in their attitudes and the way they interact with each other. Of course, fundamentalist countries have much more strict social rules, but even Western European countries have their own formalities. These should not be interpreted as unfriendliness—in many parts of the world, people are simply more cautious about shifting the status from acquaintance to friend. On the other hand, once you're in, you're in. Mariah's best friend moved to Amsterdam for grad school and had a hard time making friends at first. She didn't realize that Dutch people generally don't just nonchalantly invite you to hang out as Americans do, especially when inviting you into their homes. But she also found that when a Dutch person finally *does* invite you over for tea, they're not "just being nice," and might consider it rude not to take the invitation seriously. This means your invitations might be taken seriously, too. When Mariah took a summer course at Oxford in high school, she lived next door to a Belgian girl. They were friendly, although not really friends, but Mariah thought nothing of telling her in passing (just to be nice) that if she ever came to New York she could stay with her. Much to Mariah's surprise (and to her parents' chagrin) next December, guess what? The girl was in town and expecting to stay with her.

Another important difference is that many cultures are more physically open than ours, like Europeans or South Americans, for example. They kiss, they hug, they are close talkers, they go topless on beaches. All very strange behavior in our Puritan country, but over there, you're the one being strange. This does not mean that you should feel pressured to do anything you're not comfortable with, but boys, if a girl (or even a guy) you just met kisses you on the cheek, she (or he) is probably not flirting. Conversely, many countries are much more conservative than ours, especially in the Arab world, so keep in mind how your actions may be interpreted.

Don't bring too much baggage in general.

You have no idea how much stuff you will accumulate in a foreign country, so keep in mind you can't just load up the car and bring it all home. (Unless of course you're studying in Canada.) International shipping is expensive, and many airlines have weight restrictions for checked bags. Having too much stuff will definitely become an issue anyway, so the less you start out with the better off you'll be. On this subject Mariah has a tip, which she discovered when she went abroad to Paris. In many cases when you study abroad, you will be housed temporarily in a hostel or dorm before you find a place to live full-time. Pack a camping backpack with enough stuff for a week. That way, you can store your big suitcase somewhere safe, and not even think about it until you're ready to settle in. This little piece of advice will make the beginning of your stay remarkably more comfortable.

Don't act in ways that you wouldn't act at home.

This basic tip is the main point of most study abroad orientation lectures. Of course you're in another country, and you may not speak the language so it is easy to feel detached, but don't think that your actions won't have consequences—they will. In 2002, The U.S. Department of State issued a press release called "Travel Safety Information for Students" that addresses this issue:

> Each year, more than 2,500 American citizens are arrested abroad—about half on narcotics charges, including possession of very small amounts of illegal substances. A drug that may be legal in one country may not be legal in a neighboring nation. Some young people are victimized because they may be unaware of the laws, customs, or standards of the country they are visiting.
>
> Besides drugs, alcohol can also get U.S. citizens in trouble abroad. Students have been arrested for being intoxicated in public areas, for underage drinking, and for drunk driving. Some young Americans go abroad assuming that local authorities will overlook such conduct. Many believe that they are immune from prosecution in foreign countries because they are American citizens. The truth is that Americans are expected to obey all of the laws of the countries they visit, and those who break these laws sometimes face severe penalties, including prison sentences.

Disorderly or reckless behavior is also to be avoided. In many countries, conduct that would not result in an arrest here in the U.S. constitutes a violation of local law. It is crucial that young Americans be aware of this risk as they are enjoying their time abroad.

Another thing to remember is that as a foreigner, and especially as an American, you will stand out and potentially be an easy target. One student at a university in the Middle East said that as an American girl it is really important never to be drunk in public, because men will try to take advantage of you.

Go in for a tune-up, or "An ounce of prevention . . ."

Before you leave the country, it's a good idea to go in for all your checkups. Get full blood work done, get that root canal taken care of, make sure you're in good working order before you hop on a plane across the world. Going to the doctor is unpleasant enough as it is, and it's a much more stressful experience when the doctor does not speak English. It's no fun to get sick when you're far away from home, so try to start out healthy.

It's also a good idea to prepare all your finances before you go away. Make sure you have a reliable source of income, as it will probably be difficult (although not impossible) to support yourself by working when overseas. In fact, many countries require you to show proof of financial security before they issue you a visa. If you're going away for a long period of time, it's much more convenient to use cash cards and credit cards than it is to get traveler's checks. Make sure you check with your bank to see whether you can use your cash card and PIN in foreign machines. It's also a good idea to keep a credit card in a safe place for emergencies. One student told us that before he left to study abroad, he gave copies of all his important banking documents and customer service numbers to his dad in case his wallet was stolen (which it was). "My dad was able to facilitate the reissue of my credit cards because he had power of attorney over my finances while I was overseas and had copies of the information he needed."

Get some good advice from a reliable source.

This may seem obvious, but depending on what part of the world you're going to, speaking with someone who really knows the ropes can be vital to your comfort. When Mariah was in high school, she went on a summer program to a small island in the West Indies. Her family doctor terrified her (not to mention her already nervous mother) by telling her all sorts of crazy stories about dysentery, malaria, poisonous snakes, and man-eating piranhas. Needless to say, the recommended precautions like wearing boots into the river or sleeping fully covered in mosquito netting were a bit superfluous. An American who studied in Kenya said that before she left, a nurse told her not to drink any water, not even bottled water, and not to eat any fresh vegetables because of contamination. As a result, she became seriously dehydrated and malnourished before realizing that the water wasn't at all dangerous. It is always better to be on the safe side, and to find out as much information as possible about a place before you go there.

Always check travel and health advisories.

The U.S. Department of State publishes information on countries worldwide, including travel warnings to advise Americans of conditions abroad. These travel warnings are generally issued because of civil conflict, natural disasters, or disease outbreaks. So what does it mean if you read a warning about the country you're about to study in? Well, technically it means that you should stay the hell away, but many seasoned travelers take it as the State Department's way of saying "If you decide to go anyway, don't say we didn't warn you." There is certainly a fine line between both attitudes, so it's important to learn all the facts and then do what you feel comfortable with. Sometimes the State Department will simply issue public announcements, which are less severe than warnings. They are merely meant to alert you to issues that may concern U.S. citizens while abroad.

Travel warnings and public announcements are listed alphabetically by country on the U.S. State Department Travel Advisories web site at **http://travel.state.gov**.

The Center for Disease Control lists its own travel advisories and outbreak warnings on its web site at **www.cdc.gov/travel**.

The World Health Organization has international travel health information listed on its web site at **www.who.int/ith**.

Know what your U.S. consulate can do for you.

There are U.S. embassies in almost every major city in the world, and each has a consular section. Think of the consulate as your main resource away from home, a sort of student affairs office on a larger scale. The consular office can assist you in these specific ways:

It can issue replacement passports. This is probably what consulates are known best for, because everyone loses their passport at least once in their lifetime.

It can help you if you get sick. Consulates keep a list of appropriate doctors, dentists, and other medical specialists, and if anything serious happens to you, they can contact your family back home.

It can help you get money. Well, they can at least help you contact your family or bank, and in some cases, they can receive wire funds.

It can help you if you're arrested. If this unfortunate occurrence should befall you, ask the authorities to notify a U.S. consul. They cannot get you out of jail, but they can visit you, contact your family, help you get a lawyer, and try to get help if your human rights are being violated. (We hope you'll never need this service.)

The consular office cannot cash checks, lend you money for bail, or act as your lawyer. For a listing of U.S. embassies worldwide, go to **http://usembassy.state.gov**.

What if your family back home in the U.S. needs information in an emergency? The Office of Overseas Citizens Services in the State Department's Bureau of Consular Affairs has a 24-hour phone number: (202) 647-5225.

The OCS also has a toll-free hot line available from 8:00 A.M. to 8:00 P.M. Monday through Friday: 1-888-407-4747.

Don't worry!

As long as you keep these things in mind and make the basic preparations, you'll be OK. Almost all universities sponsor orientations upon arrival to cover the basics, like how to set up a bank account and register with the government if necessary.

HOW TO USE THIS BOOK

In the following pages, you'll find information on:

- American structured universities and colleges overseas
- Universities around the world with substantial English-language undergraduate or associate degree programs
- Select study abroad programs that we thought were especially interesting

In each profile we provide the following when available:

- Photos of the campus and facilities
- Facts and statistics about the student body and admissions
- The university's history, general mission (e.g., an American liberal arts school, Catholic school, etc.), and information about the campus and surrounding area
- Academic information such as the types of degrees offered, special programs, or core curriculum (If the college is small enough, we may list its course areas, but if a university offers too many to list, you'll have to look that up yourself using the URLs provided.)
- Information on student services, facilities, and housing
- Information on student life on and off campus

- Admissions requirements and financial information
- Contact information

Please remember that all this information may be subject to change. Many of the universities are young and growing, while others are small campuses that could possibly close on short notice. Basically, if you like what you've read about a college in our book, use the profile as a starting point to do some more research on your own.

UNDERGRADUATE
PROGRAMS

AUSTRALIA
AND NEW ZEALAND

If Crocodile Dundee and Foster's are the only things that come to mind when you think of Australia, then here's a bit about what the world's smallest continent is really like:

- Australia is the world's largest inhabited island, with a population of about 20 million. Western Australia alone is three-and-a-half times the size of Texas.
- Australia's winter starts in July, which means summer vacation is from December through February.
- No city in Australia is farther than 62 miles from the sea.

According to an Australian friend of ours, Australia is generally a very friendly country, "with a social climate that is less competitive and more forgiving than America's." She also reported that while Australia certainly has its underclass, "There is very little true poverty in the American sense, especially in the cities. This makes for a much more laid-back society, and even a different idea of what success is."

Australia has a number of different regions, all with distinctive characteristics. Said our Australian friend, "If you want sun, surf, and blonde, bronzed Australian hotties, you're better off staying away from Melbourne or Adelaide, where the weather is more temperate and the culture is less beach-crazed." Brisbane, on the other hand, is known for a great climate and some of the most beautiful beaches in Australia. If you're more of an outdoorsy type, you may want to check out Tasmania, the small island separated from mainland Australia by the 240-kilometer-wide Bass Strait—almost half of the area is uninhabited wilderness.

New Zealand, a small country a few miles south of Australia, is also known for its scenic beauty. In fact, it is so gorgeous that it doubled as the set for the mythical Middle-earth in the recent *Lord of the Rings* movie trilogy. New Zealanders, or "kiwis" as they are sometimes affectionately called (after the bird, not the fruit), are known for their love of water sports and other outdoor pursuits.

Some useful web sites:

www.studyinaustralia.gov.au—for the Australian government's official web site for international students

www.walkabout.com.au—for a comprehensive tourist guide to Australia

Australian National University
Canberra, Australia

AT A GLANCE

The Australian National University is a medium-sized research-oriented university in Australia's capital city. Students come to ANU for one of the most comprehensive Asian Studies programs offered in Australia, the personalized Engineering programs, and the superb science facilities.

> **Total Enrollment:** 10,500; 77 American
> **Undergraduate Enrollment:** 6,830
> **Male/Female:** 43/57
> **SAT Scores:** 1100 average
> **Tuition:** $7,900 per year

CAMPUS AND LOCATION

The Australian National University was established in 1946 as the country's only national research university. It has since merged with Canberra University College (in 1960) and the Institute of the Arts (in 1992) to offer many types of undergraduate and graduate programs, including creative arts and music.

Although ANU's sprawling '60s-style campus is huge, student facilities and classrooms are set close together, so it doesn't necessarily feel overwhelming. The campus is about ten minutes away from downtown Canberra, Australia's capital city. Said one Australian student, "Want to study the inner workings of the Australian Parliament? This is your town." But apart from all the politicians, Canberra is home to many museums and cultural curiosities and is also reported to be very easy to get around. Outside the city, students say that the area offers a ton of very traditional Australian activities, such as carving digerydoos, mining sapphires, and spending time on sheep ranches in the outback. Students also recommend taking a guided bus tour called the Oz Experience (**www.ozexperience.com**). Canberra is about a two-hour drive from the mountains and beaches of the south coast. Surfing in Byrom Bay is a popular pastime with ANU students, and one mentioned Nimbin as a favorite destination. For more on the city, check out **www.canberratourism.com.au**.

ACADEMICS

Students say that academics at ANU emphasize independent learning. One American visiting student felt that teaching came second to his professor's first job—conducting research in his field. Generally, students report that more time is spent studying independently and in question-and-answer sessions than in formal lectures.

ANU offers a wide array of undergraduate degrees across its six faculties—Arts, Asian Studies, Economics and Commerce, Engineering and Information Technology, Law and Science, and the National Institute of the Arts. These degrees are usually completed in three years. (Combined degrees require an extra year.) Each faculty operates like a separate college and has its own way of doing things. For example, the Faculty of the Arts offers a liberal arts–style education in which students can combine courses in a number of subjects. The Faculty of Asian Studies combines the study of an Asian language with another related major. The Faculty of Engineering is broken up into small research-and-learning groups of 20 students each.

Internship programs, which combine work experience and a related research project, are available across all faculties. ANU also has exchange programs with Oxford, Cambridge, and the University of California.

FACILITIES

ANU's main library is housed in four buildings and has five additional science branches. Its total holdings are over two million volumes. Each faculty has many of its own facilities as well. The Art Institute has its own art and photo gallery, art supply store, computer art studio, art library, music library, concert halls, recording studios, and rehearsal spaces. ANU's sports facilities include squash courts, tennis courts, rowing and sailing clubhouses, and fitness centers. ANU's student union has a game room, a small supermarket, a bakery, a dental clinic, a post office, and hairdressers. There is also an on-campus "concessions" area with a bank, a travel agency, a bookshop, cafés, and a pharmacy.

STUDENT HOUSING AND SERVICES

ANU has eight residence halls to accommodate 2,300 students. Living on campus is a very popular option. The halls are community-oriented and offer social activities and academic support in the form of organized study groups and tutorials. Many American students feel that living on campus is really the best way to experience "Aussie life," especially since the convenience factor makes it easier to be active in campus activities. All residence halls provide accommodation in single rooms with carpeting, heat, and phones with voice mail, and have computer labs, TV lounges, and laundry rooms. Some have music and art studios and common kitchens or other catering services. One student said that his favorite part of living in the dorms was getting to share a kitchen with ANU students from all over Australia, Europe, and Asia. "I really got to learn about their cultures and also got to eat lots of great, home-cooked Asian food."

American students say that the administrators and professors at ANU are very open and supportive and really help to make the transition abroad as seamless as possible for international students. The International Education Office offers a welcome orientation program each semester for international students. Academic advisory services and an academic skills and learning center provide help with writing skills and study techniques. A careers center is available for advice and guidance. There are two full-time chaplains, a 24-hour Muslim students center, four child-care centers, health services, a mental health counseling center, and a disability advisor.

CAMPUS LIFE

ANU's student union organizes many student clubs and social activities and has its own student-run radio station and newspaper. A lot of socializing goes on in the residence halls, most of which have their own pubs.

Off campus, downtown Canberra is a great place to hang out on weekends, according to students. The only complaint, or at least something that most American students needed getting used to, was that restaurants and cafés tend to close very early, especially in the winter (except for clubs, which usually stay open until at least 4 A.M.).

ADMISSIONS AND FINANCIAL INFO

Apply by December for March entry; apply by May for July entry. Each year five full-tuition scholarships are given to qualified international students. The Faculty of Engineering and Information Technology and the Faculty of Economics and Commerce offer partial scholarships to international students. International students can also apply for honors scholarships worth up to $4,000.

 CONTACTS

International Education Office
Australian National University
Pauline Griffin
Building Chancelry Annex
Elry Crescent, Acton
Canberra ACT 0200
Australia

Phone: 61-2-6125-4643
Fax: 61-2-6125-5550
E-mail: undergraduate.int@anu.edu.au
URL: www.anu.edu.au

Bond University

Queensland, Australia

AT A GLANCE

Bond University is a cozy American liberal arts university in a scenic suburban location near the beaches and mountains of southern Australia. Founded in 1987, Bond is the oldest private nonprofit university in Australia. It boasts a large international enrollment and the lowest student-to-faculty ratio of any university in Australia. Its strong Film, Television, Marketing, and Public Relations programs attract many American visiting students.

Undergraduate Enrollment: 2,300; 92 American,
1,150 other nationalities
Male/Female: 14/11
Student/Faculty: 10/1
SAT Scores: 1100 required
Tuition: approximately $20,156 per year

CAMPUS AND LOCATION

Bond's sprawling parklike campus is nestled between the mountains and the beach on Queensland's picturesque Gold Coast. The area offers attractions for nature lovers and mall rats alike. The Great Barrier Reef, famous for its diving and snorkeling, is just north of Bond, and the nearby suburbs of Robina and Lake Orr are home to a massive shopping center called Pacific Fair. Students can also head to Surfer's Paradise, an area about ten minutes away with lots of clubs, bars, and touristy shops, or make the longer drive into

Brisbane, Queensland's big capital city about an hour away. A number of theme parks are also located nearby—Seaworld, Movie World, Wet and Wild, and Dream World are all only about a half hour by car from campus.

ACADEMICS

Academics at Bond can be strenuous. The university operates on a three-semester year, so it is possible for students to earn a bachelor's degree in less than four years. The university has five main schools of study. The School of Business offers majors in Commerce or International Business, and also has a thorough and competitive internship program. The Schools of Information Technology and Law offer strong preprofessional programs. The School of Law also has an exchange arrangement with the law schools at Duke and Northwestern Universities. The School of Health Sciences (founded in 1999) is the newest at the university and offers degrees in Biomedical Science and Coaching and Sports Management. It also has a supervised preprofessional program. The School of Humanities and Social Sciences comprises many areas of study, including a new degree in Film and Television that has a professional focus.

Regardless of their school of study, all bachelor's degree candidates must take one class in each of these four core areas of study—Communication, Information Technology, Cultural and Ethical Values, and Management. Aside from its main university departments, Bond also sponsors three research centers—the Tim Fisher Center for Global Trade and Finance, the Institute for Corporate Governance, and the English Language Institute.

FACILITIES

Bond has a vast array of student facilities. The four-story main library houses over 230,000 volumes and electronic resources, and Bond also has a separate law library. The university also recently opened 15 new state-of-the-art computer labs, making the total number of computer labs on campus more than 20 (including one 24-hour lab). Its new $12 million sports center has squash and tennis courts, a soccer field, a football and rugby oval, basketball courts, a gymnasium, a 2,000-meter rowing course, and to top it off, an outdoor heated Olympic-size swimming pool. The university has a student art gallery, TV and film studios, and a pub with a performance space. It's even got its own conference and commercial center where privately owned businesses such as a coffeehouse, a physiotherapist, and a bookstore operate. Four dining halls and student cafés are located around campus.

STUDENT HOUSING AND SERVICES

Bond offers many types of on-campus accommodation. All rooms on campus are equipped with a desk, a single bed, a bedside table, a lounge chair, private phones, and high-speed internet access. In "The Towers," most rooms are doubles with a private bathroom and little closet space. One student reported that these rooms are spacious and have great views but are very quiet and unsociable. The halls of residence are supposedly much more fun and offer single rooms with a shared bathroom and common room for 5 to 12 other students. Overall, housing facilities are reported to be clean and "undingy" probably due to the fact that there is maid service and a linen change once a week. The university also has an on-campus conference center that offers hotel-type accommodations for visitors and students without housing. These rooms are equipped with private bathrooms, complimentary toiletries, TVs, radios, phones, refrigerators, and coffee machines.

Support services at Bond are comprehensive. Student counselors provide assistance with social issues and offer an optional study skills session at the beginning of each semester. Two confidential professional counselors are available for temporary aid and can refer students to more long-term outside help. Pastoral Care offers information and counseling on religious issues. Sister Valerie Evans in the medical center is available for vaccinations, contraceptive advice, first aid, and doctor and dentist referrals. She also makes house calls to students residing on campus. Students can also take advantage of the many services (including massages) available at the fitness center.

The week before the start of classes, an orientation program called "Bond Week" takes place to acclimate new students to their surroundings. Students participate in informational lectures, registration, and "meet-and-greet" dinners as well as day trips in the area. During this time and throughout the year, an international student advisor offers help with visas, work permits, and other issues.

CAMPUS LIFE

Bond University offers many chances for students to get involved in extracurricular activities through numerous student clubs and academic societies. Athletic clubs are also popular and take advantage of Bond's wonderful resources both on campus and off. They offer sports like water polo, surfing, snorkeling, and scuba diving. Students report that they feel a strong sense of community on campus, probably fostered by the beautiful surroundings. There are always students hanging out on the lawns around the man-made lake or playing impromptu volleyball games on the courts nestled between the residence halls. Also, because of its small size, students say that it is easy to meet people and make friends. One American student wrote, "The Australians are friendly and willing to help and want to become friends with the Americans." However, another visiting student complained, "There are too many Americans and many have no interest in meeting people other than Americans."

ADMISSIONS AND FINANCIAL INFO

While there are no set entry requirements, applicants are assessed based on their performance in their final two years of high school, as well as test scores and recommendations. Contact the admissions office for more details. The university does not offer any scholarships to international students.

CONTACTS

Bond University
Office of Admissions
Gold Coast QLD 4229
Australia

Phone: 61-7-5595-1111
E-mail: information@bond.edu.au
URL: www.bond.edu.au

Deakin University

Victoria, Australia

AT A GLANCE

One of the largest and most impressive of Australia's universities, Deakin is surprisingly accessible despite its size, probably due to its friendly young international representatives who can expertly help American students choose the university campus that's right for them.

> **Total Enrollment:** 25,668; 9% international
> **Undergraduate Enrollment:** 20,724
> **Male/Female:** 45/55
> **SAT Scores:** Not required
> **Tuition:** $7,671–$9,440 per year

CAMPUS AND LOCATION

Deakin is broken into a number of campuses around Victoria, Australia's second most populated state. Each has its own distinct personality and student body. The Geelong campus is Deakin's founding campus, with '70s-style architecture. Geelong is Victoria's second-largest city (pop. 200,000). It is by the bay and very close to famous surfing beaches, including Bell's Beach (Patrick Swayze's destination at the end of *Point Break*). This campus is the most "Australian" of the three main campuses and is the most popular destination for American visiting students. The student body tends to be more laid-back, and if it sounds like a cliché, often really do go to class in their board shorts. One especially enthusiastic student said, "I had intentions of going to Melbourne because it's a big city and I had heard so much about it but I am soooooo happy that I ended up in Geelong. I experienced Australia in a way the others did not."

Deakin's largest campus in Melbourne is known for a more urban, arty student body due to its location in the suburbs of the cosmopolitan Melbourne and a recent merger with the university's art school. Deakin's Warnambol campus is the smallest campus, near the commercial center of southwest Victoria and very close to the ocean. This modern campus specializes in courses in the environment, marine biology, and ecology.

ACADEMICS

Deakin is known for its innovative teaching style. The university has won the "University of the Year" award twice from Australia's *Good Universities Guide* (a major Australian college guidebook)—once in 1995 for achievements in the area of long-distance education, and again in 1999 for achievements in corporate partnerships. The university offers undergraduate degrees across five academic faculties: Arts, Business and Law, Education, Health and Behavioral Sciences, and Science and Technology, and each faculty has its own specialist schools. The university also organizes a number of internships, including a popular program in the surfing industry offered at the Geelong campus.

FACILITIES

Deakin has many state-of-the-art facilities. The library's large collection includes books, local and overseas newspapers, periodicals, CD-ROM databases, and special collections. The library also provides a range of classes and seminars to train students in research and library skills. Computer labs are open 24 hours a day. Deakin University bookshops and campus stores are located on most campuses, providing students with sundries and school memorabilia.

STUDENT HOUSING AND SERVICES

Although a bit pricey, accommodations at Deakin are thought by students to be very worthwhile. Amenities vary across the campuses from suites with shared kitchens to singles with shared common rooms and bathrooms in catered halls. One of the most popular residences is the recently completed Student Village at the Melbourne campus, which provides cushy single rooms for 200 students. Prices vary from $2,772 to $3,660 per year.

International students sometimes enjoy the freedom of being off campus. One student said that living in an apartment off campus made her feel like she was really an Australian and not just an exchange student. The university housing service can assist students in finding appropriate housing, and can also arrange homestays with families.

Deakin offers its students an incredibly wide-reaching support net, including personal and academic counseling and tutoring, and University Health Services, which provides primary health care, emergency care, and health-related counseling. Some campuses even have their own private practices. Chapels and Muslim prayer rooms are available on most campuses, and the Melbourne, Geelong, and Warnambol campus dining facilities use only Halal meat. The Career Counseling Office organizes a program to set up employers with Deakin graduates. A Women's Officer provides support for Deakin's female students and organizes meetings, workshops, and an annual campus Women's Festival. The university provides interest-free student loans of up to $1,000 through the Office of Student Life to students in good academic standing who demonstrate financial need. All students have a Deakin card, which according to the university is "your passport to the world of Deakin University." Students use this high-tech ID card to pay for just about anything on campus from laundry and vending machines to books and dining hall meals.

International students are especially well cared for. Deakin's international office arranges to meet them at the airport and sets them up with more experienced students in a host-peer partnership. Deakin also provides a three-day residential orientation program especially for exchange and study abroad students. The programs feature a range of activities like mountain biking through the pristine wilderness, guided hikes along cliff tops overlooking the Southern Ocean, surfing lessons, and workshop sessions on successful integration.

CAMPUS LIFE

Deakin University Students Association (DUSA) operates help desks that provide all sorts of services like discount movie tickets, travel info, loans, passport photos, and even free tea and coffee. DUSA organizes many special events and sponsors many student clubs. For a good tourist guide to Victoria, check out **www.visitvictoria.com**.

ADMISSIONS AND FINANCIAL INFO

Students with U.S. high school qualifications generally need one year at a recognized university to be eligible for admission. Direct entry from high school will be considered for exceptional students, or students with high AP test scores.

To help ease their education costs, international students with special visas are permitted to work part-time for up to 20 hours per week during semester and full-time during vacations.

CONTACTS

Deakin International
Deakin University
Geelong VIC 3217
Australia

Phone: 61-3-5227-1100
Fax: 61-3-5227-2001
E-mail: dconnect@deakin.edu.au
URL: www.deakin.edu.au

University of Melbourne

Melbourne, Australia

AT A GLANCE

The University of Melbourne was founded in 1885 and is one of the most prestigious and best-equipped research universities in Australia. Although it is a huge and comprehensive university, its many faculties offer the personalized attention of a small college.

Total Enrollment: 33,362; 3,947 international
Undergraduate Enrollment: 24,558
Male/Female: 50/50
Student/Faculty: 14/1
SAT Scores: Varies by faculty; most require over 1300
Tuition: $5,000 per semester

A view of the
University of Melbourne

CAMPUS AND LOCATION

The University of Melbourne's main campus at Parkville is about a 15-minute walk from downtown Melbourne, the second largest city in Australia. Home to a number of big universities, its population of over three million is made up of hundreds of thousands of students. Said one Australian, "It's a city with great food and art and music, and in some ways it's the cultural capital of Australia (although Sydney-siders will argue vehemently with that)." Melbourne is also famous for its parks and botanical gardens, as well as its cheap and efficient public transportation system (called the Met) of subways, trams, and buses. In fact, one of the only complaints about living in Melbourne is the weather—the summers are hot and the winters are cold and dreary.

ACADEMICS

The University of Melbourne has a vast academic setup; if there's something you want to study, it's probably offered here. The

Parkville campus's 13 main departments include humanities, fine arts, science, architecture, urban planning, information technology, business, engineering, education, veterinary science, agriculture, and horticulture faculties, as well as a conservatory of music and fine arts programs. The university also has interdisciplinary degree centers where students can follow combined programs, such as the Ashwood Center for Social Theory and the Center for the Study of Health and Society, where students study disease and health from a humanities perspective.

Classes are taught through lectures and seminars and assessed through exam periods at the end of the semester. Some American students found themselves having to cram like mad once exam time rolled around. Said one, "You definitely have to get used to being self-motivated when it comes to studying here."

FACILITIES

Facilities at the University of Melbourne are some of the best in the area. Its library is one of the largest in Australia with over three million volumes in 23 different branches. The Ian Potter Museum of Art on campus at Swanson Street houses a collection of 23,000 items in seven galleries and offers exhibitions, lectures, and special events. The university has its own publishing house, art museum, and movie theater, and it even runs the Melbourne Zoo. The sports center facilities include indoor and outdoor tennis courts, squash courts, a weight room, basketball and netball courts, and a track, as well as its own spa and ski lodge.

Food services consist of everything from fast-food outlets to cafeteria-style restaurants, and even a sushi bar.

STUDENT HOUSING AND SERVICES

The university offers housing at the College Square Apartments, a quick walk from campus. Apartments are managed by the YMCA and come furnished with a desk, bed, dining table, couch, refrigerator, cooktop and either a microwave or an oven, and a private bathroom. Students can choose to live alone or with one or two other people. Students pay their own electricity and water bills. Some students are also housed in ten different residential colleges, where they take all their meals and have tutorials. The university also plans to open a newly refurbished housing venue in late 2003. Students wanting to live off campus can arrange accommodations through the university.

The broad support network at the University of Melbourne includes faculty advisors, study skills helpers, medical help, and counseling. The International Student Services (ISS) department assists international students and publishes an information guide to help students adjust. There is also a Student on Arrival Assistance Program and an orientation program to help new students become comfortable on the vast campus.

CAMPUS LIFE

For University of Melbourne students, learning often continues outside the classroom. For a small fee, the university offers many extracurricular courses in academics (including languages and information technology), athletics, and fine arts and music (such as oil painting, digerydoo, and guitar). The university also schedules many free public lectures throughout the year. There is always something happening on campus. The music faculty puts on many concerts throughout the year, and the university student union organizes various events, including weekly lunchtime performances of local bands and a campus flea market.

ADMISSIONS AND FINANCIAL INFO

Admission is very selective. Students are generally required to have a 3.5 GPA, but criteria vary from course to course. Apply by December 20 for the March semester and by May 31 for the July semester.

CONTACTS

International Admissions
International Center
University of Melbourne
Victoria 3010
Australia

Phone: 61-38-3444-505
Fax: 61-39-3479-062
E-mail: unimelb@custhelp.com
URL: www.unimelb.edu.au

University of Notre Dame Australia

Fremantle, Western Australia

AT A GLANCE

Founded in 1990 as the first private Catholic university in Australia, the University of Notre Dame Australia has a study exchange with the Notre Dame in Indiana. If you're looking for an intimate, American-style education right on the beach, then this is the place for you.

Total Enrollment: 994; 60 American
Undergraduate Enrollment: 812
Male/Female: 66/34
Student/Faculty: 20/1
SAT Scores: 1000 required
Tuition: $10,920 per year
Accreditation: Australian Ministry of Education

CAMPUS AND LOCATION

The University of Notre Dame is divided into two campuses, both in Western Australia—the main undergraduate campus in Fremantle and a small campus in Broome, which was developed in 1994. Fremantle is a historical and picturesque nineteenth-century port city. The town lies on the Swan River and the Indian Ocean, and is now one of the biggest ports in Australia. It has a relaxed Mediterranean ambience and is filled with small artsy markets and coffee houses, making it the perfect university setting. The town of Broome is a small and relaxed resort town located on Australia's northwest coast. It borders beautiful beaches and the Indian Ocean. In fact, many students reported that their favorite thing about life at Notre Dame was the proximity to the beaches.

ACADEMICS

Notre Dame prides itself on giving students a "holistic" education. It emphasizes individual growth and has one of the lowest student-faculty ratios of any Australian university. Students report that academics are very competitive at Notre Dame. An average of 23 hours a week are spent in class and about 12 hours are spent doing homework. In fact, one of the few complaints students have is that their schedules are too full. Students find Notre Dame a unique and challenging place to study. The university is made up of five colleges: Business, Education, Health, Law, and Theology. The Broome campus offers programs in Nursing, Arts, and Indigenous (Aboriginal) Studies. Students are able to take double degree programs that allow them to mix areas of study.

All students follow a core curriculum their freshman year consisting of three units of ethics, theology, and law. These three areas are chosen in order to maintain a traditional liberal arts education, and also to emphasize Christian values. Notre Dame promotes "experimental" learning in all areas of study by offering a number of internship placements and volunteer work in the community. A component of practical experience is required for every degree. Students may also participate in exchanges with Notre Dame in Indiana.

FACILITIES

The campus library is small, with only about 200,000 volumes, but the university has an interlibrary loan program with the nearby Edith Cowan and Murdoch University libraries. Both campuses have computer and copy centers. The Fremantle campus offers a pub and a new bookstore.

STUDENT HOUSING AND SERVICES

Notre Dame offers many different types of accommodations. The three halls of residence for the Fremantle campus are actually located at the University of Western Australia, about 30 minutes away. Students are housed in private rooms, but must share common rooms and bathrooms. Amenities such as weekly maid service and linen change are included, as well as a 21-meal-a-week plan. Each dorm has its own laundry room, computer rooms, and sports facilities. Many students choose to live in hostels a short walk from the university. Like the dorms, these also come with single rooms and shared facilities, but meals are optional.

The university offers a number of support services. The Center for Social Ministry is an organization dedicated to upholding the moral character of the university. The center conducts research on relevant social issues, teaches Christian doctrines, and helps students develop strong community service skills. The university also runs a program called "OWLs" ("Older, Wiser Leaders"), which trains older students in assisting and welcoming the new freshman class. Each student is assigned an academic advisor or tutor, and emotional counseling is available. The Edmund Rice Center organizes volunteer work and community service activities for students and also acts as a place for students to come together and talk about their personal experiences. The campus chapel holds mass three times a week and helps promote religious life at the university. An international office helps overseas students obtain work permits and visas, and it also offers housing placement services.

CAMPUS LIFE

Notre Dame organizes a thorough range of extracurricular activities, and puts a high value on sports. The many student clubs like the debate club, Italian club, music club, and international students club, and university-wide events like frequent cocktail parties, balls, cruises, and weekend trips bolster the feeling of community on the small campus. In between classes, students can be found relaxing in the park or in the university common room. But after hours, students head to town, where The Esplanade and the Orient Hotel are reportedly two very popular Notre Dame hangouts.

ADMISSIONS AND FINANCIAL INFO

American students apply through Notre Dame International. For specific admissions requirements and scholarship opportunities, contact the international office.

 CONTACTS

Notre Dame International
16 High Street
Fremantle, WA 6160
Australia

Phone: 61-08-9433-0650
Fax: 61-08-9433-0544
E-mail: enquiries@ndi.com.au
URL: www.ndi.com.au

University of Sydney

Sydney, Australia

AT A GLANCE

The University of Sydney is Australia's oldest university, and one of its highest ranking. Since its beginnings in 1850, the university has continued to expand its facilities and services. Famous alumni include several of Australia's prime ministers, chief justices, and Aboriginal leaders. Director Jane Campion (*Sweetie, The Piano*) is a notable graduate of the Sydney College of the Arts.

> **Total Enrollment:** 42,420; 13% international
> **Undergraduate Enrollment:** 27,357
> **Student/Faculty:** 15/1
> **SAT Scores:** Required, but no minimum
> **Tuition:** $7,315–$9,308 per year

CAMPUS AND LOCATION

The Camperdown/Darlington campus is the University of Sydney's main campus. Its rolling green lawns, gothic architecture, and newly restored Edwardian Manning House lend the campus a very Ivy League air. The campus is located between the commuter suburbs of Glebe and Newton, which offer some shops, restaurants, and attractions, but for students the real excitement is just a bus ride away in downtown Sydney. This vibrant and multicultural city offers pretty much everything that a modern city should, and then some: a famous harbor, a thriving arts scene, over 30 beaches, and an alleged 342 days a year of sunshine to enjoy it all in. Said one

47

Aussie student, "If good weather and excitement are what you want, Sydney is your town. It's is kind of like Australia's L.A., but much prettier and not as dangerous. It's faster paced than Melbourne and more modern in some ways."

ACADEMICS

With over 430 different flexible undergraduate degrees across its 18 faculties and schools, the University of Sydney certainly offers something for every academic interest. Some visiting American students felt that academics were fairly laid-back compared to what they were used to in the U.S. The university also offers study abroad programs and exchanges.

FACILITIES

The University of Sydney's Fisher Library is the largest in the southern hemisphere with over 20 specialized branches, including the Schaffer Fine Arts library, known to be one of the best art libraries in Australia, as well as other art collections and galleries. The university's extensive athletics facilities include three sports centers on the main Camperdown campus, which house an aquatic center, a massive complex with weight and cardio exercise rooms, racquet sport courts, a 50-meter indoor heated pool, and a café. Sports facilities like golf courses and sports fields, a ski lodge at Thredbo in the Snowy Mountains, and boat sheds on Sydney Harbour are scattered around other university campuses. The main student center since the university's beginning, Manning House is now serving time as the university's central food and entertainment court.

STUDENT HOUSING AND SERVICES

The newly built University Village accommodates 650 students in ten apartment buildings set around a village green. Facilities range from one- to five-bedroom apartments with kitchens to single studios with shared bathrooms and no kitchens. All rooms are furnished and come with phones, voice mail, and high-speed internet connections. The Village has an indoor/outdoor dining area with different cafés and restaurants, a Village Bar (featuring an indoor BBQ pit), a convenience store, a business center, laundry facilities, and academic services. Prices range from $89 per month for a room in a shared apartment to $152 per week for a private room. (For more info visit **www.suv.com.au.**)

Residential colleges are also a popular housing option because they offer the opportunity to be a part of a close-knit community, which is rare in such a large university. Residential colleges have their own study and recreational facilities and traditions, but unlike most British residential colleges, colleges at "USyd" are not affiliated with academic programs. The university provides accommodation for only about 2,000 of their 27,000 plus students, so needless to say, most people live off campus. But in a city as large and diverse as Sydney, students have the opportunity to be a bit more creative with housing. One student told us of how she lived in an old department store that had been converted into an apartment building of sorts (albeit one without windows). The university housing offices can help students find neighborhood apartments and sublets, arrange homestays with families, and even tell students where to find thrift stores for furnishings.

The University of Sydney offers all the resources and services you would expect from such a huge university. Spiritual life is well catered to with on-campus prayer facilities for all faiths as well as a special prayer room for Muslim students on the Camperdown campus. Most student union catering outlets serve Halal food. General health care is offered at the University Health Service's clinic, and students can receive psychological counseling, academic support, career counseling, and disability services through various support offices. The University of Sydney's student union offers its own special services and benefits, like financial assistance with emergency loans of up to $1,000.

The university is especially supportive of its international students, offering them predeparture information kits, airport pickup, counseling, help finding part-time work, and even a program called UniMates which sets overseas newcomers up with Australian buddies.

CAMPUS LIFE

The University of Sydney's student union is the social backbone of the university. It is the oldest and largest student union in Australia and offers all sorts of discounts to restaurants, movies, and plays in town, sponsors over 150 student clubs, and has a number of retail stores and services as well as its own art gallery and hairdresser. Student clubs organize events and parties for their members. The Students Representative Council puts out *Honi Soit* (the weekly student paper), provides free legal advice, and runs a used bookstore.

Sports are also popular at USyd. The Sydney University Women's Sports Association (SUWSA) and the Sydney University Sports Union run over 50 clubs including American football, judo, water polo, and bushwalking. (They also boast the highest sporting achievements of any university sports club in Australia.)

ADMISSIONS AND FINANCIAL INFO

Students with American high school credentials should also have at least two AP tests and current SAT scores. Apply by October 31 for the March semester; apply by April 30 for the July semester.

American students are advised to make applications through a university representative office.

 CONTACTS

International Office
University of Sydney
Services Building G12
NSW 2006
Australia

Continues ☞

Phone: 61-2-9351-4079/4161
Fax: 61-2-9351-4013
E-mail: furtherinfo@io.usyd.edu.au
URL: www.usyd.edu.au

Australian Education Connection
5722 South Flamingo Road, #303
Cooper City, FL 33330-3206

Phone: 954-680-0453
Toll-free: 800-565-9553
Fax: 954-680-0597
E-mail: AustStudy@aol.com

Study Australia L. C.
1200 Wales Avenue
Birmingham AL 35213

Phone: 205-956-8265
Fax: 205-357-9457
E-mail: info@study-australia.com

University of Tasmania

Tasmania, Australia

AT A GLANCE

One of Australia's oldest and most respected universities, the University of Tasmania offers generous scholarships to international students. Many American students come for its flexible academic structure, which allows them to combine programs across different faculties, such as Fine Arts with Wilderness Studies (two of the most popular courses).

Total Enrollment: 12,000; 1,200 international
Undergraduate Enrollment: 10,830
Male/Female: 44/56
Student/Faculty: 22/1
SAT Scores: Not required
Tuition: approximately $7,073 per semester

CAMPUS AND LOCATION

The University of Tasmania was founded in Hobart in 1890, as the fourth university in Australia, and to this day is the only university in Tasmania. It has two major campuses, the main one in Hobart and a smaller one in Launceston, as well as a study center in Burnie, on the island's northwest coast. Tasmania is a safe, beautiful, and clean place to live, and although over half of the small island (about the size of Ireland) is a wilderness park, Tasmania's vibrant culture and academic community keeps it from being just a "backwater 'burb." In the cities, there are plenty of things to see and do, and a great public transportation system to get you there.

U Tas's main campus is on 200 acres of beautifully landscaped grounds a few miles from downtown Hobart, Tasmania's capital city. As a maritime city, Hobart's sandstone Georgian buildings, markets, and cafés are set around the docks of the Derwent River, a large estuary fed by the Southern Ocean. Hobart's rich cultural scene offers all types of art, music, and theater. For those who want to get away from it all, the city is just a short drive to the slopes of Mt. Nelson and Mt. Wellington.

ACADEMICS

Academics are strong at U Tas. Students report that most classes are small, and the professors are friendly and approachable. The university offers undergraduate degrees across its seven faculties: Arts, Commerce, Education, Health Science, Law, Science, and Engineering and Technology. There are also a number of Tasmania-specific courses offered like Aquaculture, Wilderness Management, and Antarctic and South Ocean Studies.

FACILITIES

The university library comprises six libraries in Hobart and one in Launceston, as well as an information resources area in the Northwest Center at Burnie. Other university-run facilities include the Tasmanian Conservatorium of Music and the Center for the Arts. The Union Building at Hobart houses a cafeteria (The Refectory), a bar, a general store, a bookstore, a hairdresser, a post office, a copy service (The Contact Center), a travel agent, bank branches, and the student health service. The sports and recreation center offers tennis and volleyball courts, weight rooms, indoor and outdoor climbing walls, and an indoor soccer and rugby field.

STUDENT HOUSING AND SERVICES

The Hobart campus offers housing in residential colleges. This type of accommodation usually appeals to American visiting students who like the fact that it's easier to make friends with Tasmanian students when living with them. All colleges are coed with single bedrooms and shared bathrooms. Other housing options include shared houses, which are only available on the Hobart campus. These accommodate students in single bedrooms in a suite with two to four other students with a shared kitchen, bathroom, and common room. The accommodation officer can also arrange homestays with Tasmanian families who have been carefully selected.

U Tas provides health services and academic and personal support from tutors, psychologists, and social workers. The international student office organizes an orientation for overseas students. Other services include career counseling and religious support.

CAMPUS LIFE

The student body at U Tas is generally described as being liberal and involved. The student union also organizes many academic, cultural, and recreational clubs for those less physically inclined. The uniquely untouched natural beauty of Tasmania inspires many students to head for the great outdoors, and university clubs can supply any type of equipment you would need for sports like white-water rafting, bushwalking, and surfing remote beaches.

ADMISSIONS AND FINANCIAL INFO

American high school credentials are generally sufficient to be considered for admission. Scholarships based on academic achievement are available to all undergraduate students and provide 25% off tuition fees for the entire course, including honors years.

CONTACTS

International Admissions and Exchanges
University of Tasmania
P.O. Box 252-38
Hobart
Tasmania 7001
Australia

Phone: 61-3-6226-2706
Fax: 61-3-6226-7862
E-mail: S.Lacey@utas.edu.au
URL: www.international.utas.edu.au

University of Waikato

Hamilton, New Zealand

AT A GLANCE

The University of Waikato is a large university in a small college town known for being one of the most beautiful campuses in all of New Zealand. The university also has the distinction of having the most Maori (the country's indigenous people) students in all of New Zealand.

55

Total Enrollment: 13,000; 1,100 international
Undergraduate Enrollment: 11,400
Male/Female: 46/54
Student/Faculty: 18/1
SAT Scores: Required, but no minimum
Tuition: $7,719 per year

CAMPUS AND LOCATION

The University of Waikato's green landscaped campus is near downtown Hamilton, the north island of New Zealand's largest city with a population of only 100,000. As the urban mecca of New Zealand (which isn't saying all that much), Hamilton has decent shopping and dining areas (Metropolis café and Bazurk's for "yummy pizza, drinks, and dessert"), as well as a number of summer festivals and cultural events, like the Balloons Festival, Hamilton Gardens Summer Festival, and the Festival of the Environment. (For more about the city visit **www.hamiltoncity.co.nz**.)

As in most of New Zealand, outdoor activities and water sports are especially popular pastimes. Students enjoy exploring the Waitomo Caves about 40 minutes from Hamilton, and say that Raglan on the west coast offers great surfing. Many students think that the best thing about Hamilton isn't necessarily the city itself, but its central location. Students suggest seeing as much of New Zealand as possible. Said one, "It may be a small country, but it is packed full with heaps of crazy and beautiful places. I still have a list of things I want to come back and do!"

ACADEMICS

Waikato offers a large number of bachelor's degrees, and stresses the flexible nature of its undergraduate programs. The undergraduate degree usually takes three years to complete and is made up of "papers" (or subjects) taught at different levels of advancement. Students organize their own schedule of lectures, tutorials, and labs.

For first-year papers, you are generally expected to have two lectures and one tutorial a week, or about 40 hours of work. To gain a better appreciation of the country, American visiting students recommend taking an introductory Maori class, a basic course on the culture and beliefs of the indigenous peoples of the region.

FACILITIES

Waikato's library system is made up of three libraries with total holdings of over one million volumes. Its performing arts complex houses four performance spaces, and other facilities for music and dance are spread out across the campus. The rec center offers a vast array of athletic, aerobic, and weight training facilities as well as two pools, racquet courts, and various physical therapy and massage treatments.

HOUSING AND STUDENT SERVICES

Waikato has a number of residence halls to accommodate students in various styles. For example, College Hall and the Student Village are self-catered and offer similar amenities, and have Kaupapa Maori floors for students who want to be immersed in Maori culture. Another residence, Orchard Park, is self-catered and made up of four- to six-bedroom cottages. All residences have a live-in staff, housekeeping services, computer labs, student lounges, copy and fax facilities, and TV rooms with vending machines. Residences also organize sporting and social events like the Annual Ball and Formal Dinner. Most students who live on campus enjoy the fact that it allows them more opportunity to mingle with their international peers, and also find it easier to get their homework done in a dorm environment where everyone else is studying, too.

Waikato offers full health and counseling services at its medical center, which even has its own pharmacy. Other support services are provided through the international student counselor, disability support services, and the ecumenical chaplain. (The university's Catholic priest conducts mass three days a week.) The Teaching and Learning Development Unit (TLDU) offers workshops for students to improve their communication, math, and study skills.

CAMPUS LIFE

Students generally have few complaints about life at Waikato, but some visiting international students expressed the hope that "in the future the university will involve the international students more in the student union activities and functions." The student union at Waikato is an active one, sponsoring student clubs and organizing festivals and live music throughout the year as well as an introductory event at the beginning of the year for new students. The union also has two student bars and one of them, the Hillcrest, is actually thought to be one of the best nightspots in the area.

ADMISSIONS AND FINANCIAL INFO

Apply by December 1 for March entry and May 1 for July entry. The student recruitment team organizes events like information day and meets one-on-one with prospective students to answer questions about life at Waikato. For more information, e-mail **recruitment@waikatio.ac.nz**. The university does not offer any scholarships to international students.

 CONTACTS

International Center
University of Waikato
Private Bag 3105
Hamilton
New Zealand

Phone: 64-7-838-4439
Fax: 64-7-838-4267
E-mail: international@waikato.ac.hz
URL: www.waikato.ac.nz

BULGARIA

American University in Bulgaria
Blagoevgrad, Bulgaria

AT A GLANCE

A small American liberal arts college in a Bulgarian metropolis, the American University in Bulgaria is considered the best university in the area and offers especially strong Business Administration and Political Science/International Relations majors.

Undergraduate Enrollment: 750; 33% international
Male/Female: 45/55
Student/Faculty: 15/1
SAT Scores: 1240 required
Tuition: $12,050 per year
Accreditation: New England Association of Schools and Colleges, Bulgarian Ministry of Education

CAMPUS AND LOCATION

The American University in Bulgaria was founded in 1991 by the Republic of Bulgaria and a grant from the U.S. Agency of International Development. The modern-looking wooded campus is located in the center of Blagoevgrad (population 70,900), the economic and cultural capital of southwest Bulgaria. Nestled between the Rila and Pirin mountain ranges, with a Mediterranean climate, Blagoevgrad is quiet, safe, and clean. One of its main attractions is a tenth-century monastery, and it also offers many shops, cafés, and bars. The two movie theaters in town show mainly American movies (not dubbed), and there's also a decent video store. Blagoevgrad has its own theater and opera house, but one student said that very few productions come to town, and they seldom change. Students often head to the larger town of Sofia, about one and a half hours away, when they've exhausted Blagoevgrad's possibilities.

ACADEMICS

Academics are strenuous and requirement-heavy at AUBG. The first year starts with core courses in computer skills, composition, and statistics. Students must also take the Writing Across the Curriculum (WAC) program, which is made up of three Writing Intensive Courses (WICs), one of which must be taken in a student's major. In addition to the WAC program, students have to fulfill general education requirements, consisting of 12 courses in 7 different areas outside of a student's major. Majors are offered in about 13 different areas, the most popular one being Business.

FACILITIES

Most of AUBG's facilities and offices are located in the university's main building, which houses a library with over 100,000 volumes in English as well as a restaurant and café, both popular student hangouts. New facilities are currently being built to accommodate the growing student body. AUBG also has many computer labs as well as a multimedia lab offering digital video editing and other tools.

STUDENT HOUSING AND SERVICES

All AUBG students live in the brand-new, cushy Skaptopara residence hall, which is within walking distance of the main campus.

American University in Bulgaria's
newly built Skaptopara dorm complex

This complex houses students in double and triple rooms in two- to three-person suites with internet connections as well as resident advisors and 24-hour security guards. Other amenities include laundry rooms, two gyms, pool and Ping-Pong rooms, study lounges, three TV lounges, two computer labs, a screening room, a digital photo lab, and an outdoor area with basketball courts and soccer fields.

For such a small university, AUBG offers a wide range of student support. Orientation at the beginning of the year helps new students adjust to college life, and throughout the year students receive counseling and support via the health center, the campus living office, and the careers office.

CAMPUS LIFE

AUBG has many student clubs and offers organized activities like regional trips, an annual arts festival, intramural sports, and community service programs. The student government sponsors newspapers, magazines, a radio station, and an award-winning choir and student theater group. Students at AUBG are reportedly more into working than playing. Said one student, "People are so involved in studying that most of them forget about their social life!" But some do manage to find time to party in town—a club called Underground is said to be packed with AUBG students on Thursday nights.

ADMISSIONS AND FINANCIAL INFO

Applicants are required to have a 3.0 GPA. Apply by June 1 for the fall semester and November 1 for spring. The admissions office recommends applying early to increase your chances of getting in.

 CONTACTS

Seth Payer or Benjamin Williams
Assistant Directors of International Recruitment
American University in Bulgaria
Blagoevgrad 2700
Bulgaria

Phone: 359-73-23644
Fax: 359-73-80174
E-mail: admissions@aubg.bg
URL: www.aubg.bg

CANADA

A little bit cleaner than the U.S., a little bit safer, maybe even a little bit better—no wonder a UN survey in the '90s found Canada to be the best place in the world to live. For any further arguments on why Canada is a nice place to live, watch social pundit Michael Moore's documentary *Bowling for Columbine*—you just might want to move to the country where people don't lock their doors at night (or shoot each other).

Did you know:

- Canada has two official languages—French and English. About 3.1% of its population is francophone (French-speaking).
- The educational system is much more egalitarian than America's—70% of education costs in Ontario are subsidized by the government.
- Canada is cheaper. The U.S. dollar is still stronger than the Canadian dollar, so it's like a giant countrywide 30% off sale all the time!

Some useful web sites:

www.studyincanada.com—for information about the Canadian educational system
www.cic.gc.ca—for immigration information
www.canadiangreeks.com—for a guide to Canadian chapters of national fraternities and sororities

Bishop's University

Lennoxville, Quebec

AT A GLANCE

Looking to study in francophone Quebec, but intimidated by the gigantic McGill University? Well you might want to check out its small-town neighbor, Bishop's, a much cozier university that emphasizes student-teacher relationships and student involvement.

Total Enrollment: 1,900; 6.5% American
Undergraduate Enrollment: 1,885
Male/Female: 43/57
Student/Faculty: 13/1
SAT Scores: 1100 required
Tuition: $5,639 per year

CAMPUS AND LOCATION

Bishop's was founded in 1845 on 550 acres of manicured lawns, gardens, and stately trees. Gazebos and ivy-covered limestone buildings give the Heritage-style campus an old-world New England air, although the university is located in Lennoxville, a small francophone region of Quebec in the eastern townships. The region offers some of the best outdoor sporting activities in Canada, and is close to Montreal and its American border states, Vermont, New Hampshire, and Maine.

ACADEMICS

Bishop's is known for its small class sizes, which allow students to foster relationships with their professors. First-year courses generally have about 40 students, while in the final year the average drops to about 15. Undergraduate degrees are offered from departments in the Williams School of Business and Economics, the School of Education, the Divisions of Humanities, Natural Sciences and Mathematics, and the Social Sciences, and include many interdisciplinary programs.

FACILITIES

The John Bassett Memorial Library houses a nice-sized collection, and new computer labs around campus and the main Cole Computer Center boast one computer to every ten students and a laptop leasing program.

Bishop's is home to the Centennial Theatre, a 600-capacity theater with a smaller studio theater in the round. Bandeen Hall is a 156-seat recital hall in a beautifully restored nineteenth-century building. The university art gallery shows contemporary and historical exhibitions and hosts lectures and film screenings. The Curry Wildlife Refuge on campus is a large wetland conservation area and teaching lab. As for sports facilities, the campus offers a sports complex featuring tennis and squash courts, indoor and outdoor pools, gymnastics, weights, martial arts, and dance studios. Bishop's runs the Old Lennoxville Golf Club, a nine-hole course on campus, and also maintains cross-country ski trails and bike paths, a prestigious sports medicine facility, and playing fields, including Coulter Field, a 3,000-seat football stadium.

The university center is the hub of student life on campus. Located in three newly renovated buildings, the center houses student government club offices and meeting rooms, the bookstore, Gaiter Grill, The Loft and the Pub, the mail room, student services offices, and the international center.

STUDENT HOUSING AND SERVICES

Bishop's six residence halls accommodate about 500 students on campus. Each has live-in resident assistants, and laundry facilities, study rooms, TV lounges, and other common areas with vending machines. Students living in residences must be on one of the three meal plans.

Student services at Bishop's are all-encompassing. They include a writing center and peer tutoring service, a career placement center, counseling and health services, and chaplaincy.

CAMPUS LIFE

Bishop's student body is very involved, especially when it comes to sports. Students paint their faces purple and come out in droves at homecoming to support their beloved Gaiters. (Visit **www.fan.ca/network/gaiters** for the official web site of Bishop's sports teams.) Bishop's University offers many intramural sports and six intercollegiate sports: men's and women's alpine skiing, men's and women's golf, men's and women's basketball, men's and women's rugby, men's football, and women's soccer. The Students' Representative Council manages campus recreational facilities, and backs a number of student clubs and organizations like the Pink Triangle club, a student store, a radio station, a literary magazine, and a campus newspaper.

ADMISSIONS AND FINANCIAL INFO

Bishop's is relatively selective, and a 3.5 GPA is required for acceptance. Apply by March 1 for fall term. Limited need-based financial aid may be available for international students. Once accepted, international students may also apply for merit-based tuition reductions. Students with French citizenship, or those who enroll in a French program, may be eligible for discounted tuition.

CONTACTS

International Student Office
Bishop's University
Lennoxville, Quebec J1M 1Z7
Canada

Phone: 819-822-9600
Fax: 819-822-9661
E-mail: liaison@ubishops.ca
URL: www.ubishops.ca

Dalhousie University

Halifax, Nova Scotia

AT A GLANCE

As the self-proclaimed "smallest of Canada's big universities," Dalhousie University (affectionately known as "Dal") offers a wide array of majors and extracurricular activities in a friendly and personal atmosphere. Located right on the Atlantic, the university also offers an especially strong Marine Biology program.

CANADA

```
Total Enrollment: 15,000; 1,100 overseas, 40 American
Undergraduate Enrollment: 8,000
Male/Female: 48/52
SAT Scores: 1100 required
Tuition: $6,233 per year
```

CAMPUS AND LOCATION

Dalhousie University was initially founded in 1818 by Lord Dalhousie but closed down soon after, reopening 50 years later in 1863 as a restructured version of the original university. In 1997, Dalhousie took over the Technical University of Nova Scotia (now known as DalTech), turning it into the Faculty of Computer Science. The university's main campus is located on 60 acres of manicured green campus sandwiched between the Atlantic Ocean and downtown Halifax. Halifax is the cultural and economic center of Nova Scotia, a vibrant and cozy (although very rainy) eighteenth-century port city. A university town, Halifax is a hotbed of youth culture. For information on the city's growing club, rave, and underground art and music scene, visit **www.highway7.com**.

ACADEMICS

Dalhousie offers a wide range of undergraduate programs across its faculties of Architecture (including Urban and Rural Planning), Arts and Social Sciences, Computer Science, Dentistry, Engineering, Graduate Studies, Health Professions, Law, Management, Medicine, Science, and Henson College (regional economic, social, and cultural development). Ocean Studies and Health Studies are reported to be especially strong courses, and Journalism and Law are two of the university's more popular minors. All students are required to participate in a co-op program which entails three months of full-time paid work in a field related to their major.

Canada's Dalhousie University

FACILITIES

Dalhousie's main academic facility is the Killam Library, which has computer labs in the basement and its own snack bar, the Killam Library Atrium. Dal's arts facilities are a bit more varied. The arts center is made up of the Rebecca Cohn Auditorium, the Sir James Dunn Theatre, the David McMurray Studio, and the Dalhousie art gallery, which regularly hosts exhibits by local, national, and international artists. Sports facilities at the Studley Gym and Dalplex, the main athletic complex, include a pool, a climbing wall, a golf driving cage, a dance studio, and weight training and fitness rooms.

STUDENT HOUSING AND SERVICES

Dalhousie offers a number of types of student accommodation from traditional dorms to university-owned houses and apartment complexes for senior students. All of Dalhousie's residence rooms offer internet hook-up and TV lounges. Some have shared kitchens, but since students in residence are required to be on the meal plan, most eat at the Howe Hall dining room and enjoy not having to cook for themselves. The off-campus housing office provides students with information to help them find local housing. Students recommend looking for off-campus apartments north of the downtown area. Room and board costs are about $3,800 per year.

Dal provides support services in the way of a health clinic, a women's center, a student advocacy service, career counseling, chaplaincy, a writing workshop, and security escorts for students at night.

CAMPUS LIFE

The Dalhousie student union is very active on campus, organizing many recreational and political activities year-round, starting with Frosh Week, an orientation each fall giving new students an opportunity to get involved in the school. Whether it be having a drink at Grawood, the student union pub, or hanging out in town, students enjoy the sense of community both on campus and off. One said, "You cannot go anywhere without running into someone you know." Sports are popular, and when the Dalhousie Tigers, Dal's beloved soccer team, play home games at Wickwire field, the stands are packed. The campus radio station, CKDU-FM, is the area's major alternative music radio station and helped spawn the career of Sarah McLachlan, a Halifax native.

ADMISSIONS AND FINANCIAL INFO

While there are no officially stated entry requirements, applicants are expected to have a B average. Some need-based scholarships may be available to American students.

CONTACTS

Office of the Registrar
Dalhousie University
Halifax, Nova Scotia
Canada B3H 3JS

Phone: 902-494-2450
Fax: 902-494-1630
E-mail: admissions@dal.ca
URL: www.dal.ca

Glendon College, York University

Toronto, Ontario

AT A GLANCE

Glendon College is the small bilingual liberal arts faculty of Toronto's well-respected York University. Glendon offers a personalized education with a focus on public affairs, unique in that its classes are offered in both French and English.

Undergraduate Enrollment: 2,000
Male/Female: 30/70
Student/Faculty: 20/1
SAT Scores: 1100 required
Tuition: $7,308 per year

CAMPUS AND LOCATION

Glendon was founded in the early '60s as an offshoot of York University, one of Ontario's larger, more reputable universities. Its campus was built on the converted 85-acre summer property of an early-twentieth-century financier, in an upscale suburban neighborhood of Toronto. The campus was originally York's main campus until the parent university moved to a larger campus in 1966 (known as the Keele campus from its street address), about 20 minutes away from Glendon. A shuttle connects Glendon and York, which share some facilities and resources.

ACADEMICS

Glendon is the only bilingually integrated college in Canada. In other bilingual universities, the English and French faculties are separate, and students must declare a language of study. At Glendon, students can go back and forth freely between classes taught in either language. This aspect of the Glendon education is central to the college's academic mission, which is to educate Canada's future leaders. To reflect this purpose, all college professors, administrators, and staff can function in both languages. But if you decide you don't want to pursue French, you don't really have to—the bilingual requirements are not especially taxing. In order to graduate, students are required to take only one language course at the sophomore-year level. Students choose classes in English or French from 21 degree programs leading to a B.A. and from many other certificate programs designed to augment the B.A.

Many programs are multidisciplinary (for example, International Studies, Canadian Studies, Psychology, Environment and Health Studies) and all students must take a number of elective courses outside their major. Students also have the option of taking classes at other faculties within York, and sometimes at other nearby Canadian universities.

Classes are taught mainly through lectures with Q&A sessions and tutorials in the early years, but as students reach their upper years the classroom setting becomes more intimate, culminating with mainly seminars in the final year.

FACILITIES

Glendon's campus has its own library with a large bilingual collection and state-of-the-art computer labs. Sports facilities include a swimming pool, squash courts, an indoor driving range, dance studios, and outdoor running, hiking, and cross-country skiing trails. Athletic services include spinning classes, massage therapy, a foot-care clinic, and a physiotherapy clinic. Students also have use of the many facilities at York's nearby Keele campus.

STUDENT HOUSING AND SERVICES

Glendon's residences house about 400 students in a variety of accommodations. A few dorms have kitchens, but preference for these is given to senior students or students with special dietary needs. All other students are required to be on the meal plan since Glendon considers the dining hall experience to be crucial in fostering the sense of community on campus. As far as dining options go, students can choose from the cafeteria, the student-run Café de la Terrace, or the sports lounge. Room and board ranges from $3,068 to $3,972 per year. All non-Canadian students are guaranteed a place on campus their first year.

Glendon takes pride in the amount of support that it gives its foreign students. International student services holds an orientation before the start of classes, and the new students' airport welcome orientation package comes with a Canadian dollar to use in the airport luggage cart machine. The advising office gives year-round academic support, while the office of student programs advises solely upper-year students. Students may also participate in various seminars and tutorials to improve their study skills. The campus has its own chaplaincy and a foot-care and physiotherapy clinic, but with a large hospital nearby there is no need for health service facilities on campus.

CAMPUS LIFE

Glendon's involved student body contributes to the small college's strong sense of community. The campus has its own theater, art gallery, biweekly newspaper, and radio station. The Glendon College student union sponsors many academic and cultural student clubs, including a gay and lesbian club and an international student club.

ADMISSIONS AND FINANCIAL INFO

Students apply directly to York, which is a highly selective university. Applicants are required to have completed high school with at least a 3.0 GPA. Apply by March 1 for September entry, October 1 for January entry.

Some merit scholarships are offered to international students each year, and American students may be eligible for work-study programs. Jobs are posted in the early fall on **www.campus worklink.com**.

 ## CONTACTS

Liaison Office
Glendon Campus
C102 York Hall
2275 Bayview Avenue
Toronto, Ontario M4N 3M6
Canada

Phone: 416-487-6710
Fax: 416-487-6813
E-mail: liaison@glendon.yorku.ca
URL: www.glendon.yorku.ca

McGill University

Montreal, Quebec

AT A GLANCE

McGill is one of the most prestigious universities in Canada and it's located in one of the most interesting cities in North America. With a very large international student body, it also has the highest number of Rhodes Scholars of any Canadian university. One student summed up the university by saying, "McGill is a large community made up of many smaller ones. You will shape your own McGill experience by the faculty you choose, the courses you select, the friends you meet, the sports you play, and the residence or area in which you live—not to mention the way you tap into Montreal."

Total Enrollment: 30,000
Undergraduate Enrollment: 21,544; 5% American,
    11.6% other nationalities
Male/Female: 40/60
Student/Faculty: 10/1
SAT Scores: 1200 required
Tuition: $6,800–$10,770 per year

CAMPUS AND LOCATION

In 1813, Scottish immigrant-turned-businessman James McGill died and left a large sum of money to found the "Royal Institute for the Advancement of Learning" (now McGill University) on his 46-acre estate for the education of Quebec's English-speaking population. In 1907, the university added the Macdonald campus about 25 miles west of Montreal at Ste-Anne-de-Bellevue, which is today the site of McGill's Faculty of Agricultural and Environmental Sciences.

McGill's large downtown campus (over 70 buildings across 80 landscaped acres) is located at the foot of Mount Royal Park and its gates open onto downtown Montreal's commercial district and its many restaurants, cafés, high-rises, boutiques, and the world's largest underground shopping mall, a great place to hide out when the winter months bring subfreezing temperatures. With a population of over three million, Montreal is one of the largest francophone cities in the world, combining both the French and the English traditions of Canada. It is distinctly North American (think hockey, football, beer, and rugged individualism) with a very European atmosphere, especially in the "Veille Ville," or the old city, where most people still speak only French. The rest of Montreal is laid out around the scenic Mount Royal Park, and is thought to be very pedestrian-friendly although it has a good public transit system. Including McGill, there are four universities in Montreal, and its student population is over 100,000.

ACADEMICS

Academics at McGill are challenging, as would be expected at such a prestigious institution. Students report that they really have to "fight for every mark," which is seen as a good thing, but they also say that although course work and lectures are demanding, the exams are generally not that hard. McGill offers a vast array of study options across its 11 faculties (Agricultural and Environmental Sciences, Arts, Dentistry, Education, Engineering, Law, Management, Medicine, Music, Religious Studies, and Science) and undergraduate programs in 7 of its 10 schools (Architecture, Computer Science, Dietetics and Human Nutrition, Environment, Nursing, Physical and Occupational Therapy, Social Work, and the Institutes of Air and Space Law, Comparative Law, Islamic Studies, and Parasitology). Most faculties can help students organize internships at prestigious companies, and the Engineering and Science faculties have a program called the Internship Year for Engineering and Science (IYES), in which companies employ students for 8- to 16-month periods offering both degree credit and a salary.

McGill has exchange agreements with 500 schools around the world, open to all full-time sophomore students with a minimum 3.0 GPA, and it also organizes many of its own study abroad programs. Students say that McGill is a great place to go to learn French. French is the mother tongue of one in five McGill students, and term papers and exams may be written in French.

FACILITIES

McGill offers some of Canada's most comprehensive learning facilities, including 17 libraries, 6 teaching hospitals, and many other resources, including the Morgan Arboretum and Herbarium, the Avian Science and Conservation Center, the Ecomuseum, the Stoneycroft Wildlife Area, the Macdonald Farm, and McGill's Gault Nature Reserve at Mont St-Hilaire, as well as research stations in the Arctic, Bermuda, and New Brunswick. Several museums are also affiliated with McGill, including the McCord Museum of Canadian History, Redpath Museum of Natural History, Lyman Entomological Museum, and the McGill Archives.

The Shatner Building, also called the University Center, is the epicenter of student life, housing many recreational and dining facilities like Gert's Bar and Caférama (featuring two big-screen TVs and a smoking section) as well as a food court on the second floor. Students report that the food at McGill is especially good since the university has its own food services department and doesn't use an outside catering agency as most schools do. Shatner is also home to University Bytes, the campus discount computer store; Travel Cuts, a travel agency that helps students plan cheap, "kick-ass" vacations; and Sadie's, the student-run general store and snack shop.

McGill is very well equipped when it comes to sports facilities. The McConnell Winter Arena is the university's ice hockey rink, and Molson Stadium is home to McGill's intercollegiate football, soccer, and field hockey teams as well as to the Alouettes, Montreal's team in the Canadian Football League. The state-of-the-art sports medicine

CANADA

clinic is widely renowned and provides its services to McGill students
and staff, as well as to professional athletes and the general public.
The McGill sports center, located conveniently near the main campus
and student residences, houses many sports and recreational facilities.

STUDENT HOUSING AND SERVICES

McGill's large cinder-block dorms (sometimes referred to as the
"student ghetto") accommodate 1,700 students, with mainly first-
year but also some upper-year student leaders in residence. Each
residence hall has a live-in support network made up of a Director/
Warden, Assistant Director/Assistant Warden, and Floor-fellows/
Dons. Students live in double and single rooms with internet access
provided through McGill's student telephone service.

The residences are described as being "unpleasantly like most
other university dorms . . . too hot and too cold at the most inap-
propriate times of year." However, most students do seem to enjoy
the convenience of living on campus because of its proximity to the
city's main party streets.

McGill offers a wide range of support services, including international student services, insurance, orientation, financial assistance, housing, tutoring, crisis support, a health clinic, personal/
psychological counseling, a women's center, and legal services. One
student told us that he felt that McGill's services are merely "a
token," but on the other hand, he said, "University services that are
lacking are made up for by student organizations monitored and
coordinated by the deans."

The first-year office helps students get through orientation and
registration, which can be truly daunting at the huge university.

CAMPUS LIFE

A thriving social scene combined with rigorous academics make for
what one student describes as "the (im)balance between work and
play, a pretty intense experience."

McGill students find many ways to get involved in the community, through student clubs (the most popular ones being the De-

bating Union, UNSAM [Model United Nations], the Sexual Assault Center, Walksafe, and Queer Group). There is also a radio station, CKUT-FM, and various student publications. Sports are very big at McGill, with over 700 intramural teams and varsity teams.

The Players' Theatre is a student-run production space with a 200-seat capacity. It hosts events throughout the year, the most important of which is the McGill Drama Festival. Gert's bar/nightclub, located in the basement of the Shatner Building, has a daily happy hour from 4 to 7 P.M. and throws a weekly party known as Thursday Night Tradition (TNT), reported to be "one of the best parties in Montreal." One student remarked, "How many other bars are open early enough that you can go have a drink after your morning exam?"

ADMISSIONS AND FINANCIAL INFO

McGill is definitely a tough school to get into, and students are required to have a 3.5 GPA for admission.

Scholarship opportunities are limited for international students, but American students may be eligible to participate in the university's work-study programs.

CONTACTS

Recruitment and Registrar's Office
McGill University
845 Sherbrooke Street West
Montreal, Quebec H3A 2T5
Canada

Phone: 514-398-6424
Fax: 514-398-8939
E-mail: admissions@mcgill.ca
URL: www.mcgill.ca

Queen's University

Kingston, Ontario

AT A GLANCE

Located on the north shore of Lake Ontario in Kingston, Queen's is one of the most prestigious universities in Canada. It is also the only university in North America to offer a program in biomedical computing. Queen's history of academic excellence, school spirit, and strong athletic tradition have earned it the nickname "Harvard of the Northeast."

Total Enrollment: 18,649; 5% international
Undergraduate Enrollment: 12,703
Male/Female: 45/55
SAT Scores: 1200 required
Tuition: $7,919–$11,094 per year (non-Canadian students)

CAMPUS AND LOCATION

Founded in 1841, Queen's was modeled after the University of Edinburgh and is proud of its Scottish heritage. It is a historical school, home to Canada's first session of parliament, and its old stone buildings and oak tree–lined walkways give the campus a very traditional feel. The university also has a small study abroad campus in southern England, the International Study Center at Herstmonceaux Castle.

The campus is about a ten-minute walk from the center of Kingston, one of Canada's oldest cities. With two other universities in the area, Kingston is a small college town (population 14,000), which students report is cozy but can sometimes feel stifling. For more info on the "limestone city" (so nicknamed for its buildings), check out **www.kingstoncanada.com**.

ACADEMICS

Academics at Queen's are considered to be very strong across all faculties. The Faculty of Arts and Sciences offers the most breadth to its degrees, which are made up of a concentration and electives that can be chosen from any department. The university offers hundreds of undergraduate degree programs across its Faculties of Arts and Sciences, Applied Sciences (with a 30% female enrollment, it has more women students than any other engineering school in Canada), Business Education, Health Sciences, and the Theological College. The teaching level at Queen's is reported to be extremely high. Students evaluate teachers each year through a system called "Quest" (Queen's University Evaluation System for Teaching), which helps ensure that the award-winning professors and visiting scholars don't rest on their laurels. First-year courses do tend to be large, and are sometimes taught by TAs, but get smaller as the years go up. Two hundred intensive yearlong (paid!) internships are available to qualified students in commerce, computing, and engineering programs.

All Queen's students are eligible to take courses at the International Study Center in East Sussex, England (about 60 miles south of London). The center, which is housed in a fifteenth-century Norman castle on a 550-acre estate in the English countryside, includes a library, computing and athletic facilities, a school shop, a dining hall, and the Headless Drummer pub. Students can attend the international study center as early as freshman year. Queen's also has study abroad exchanges with over 70 universities worldwide.

FACILITIES

Cultural and research facilities at Queen's are numerous. They include a vast library system in the $42 million Joseph Stauffer Library, a $52 million Bioscience Complex, and a new chemistry complex said to be the largest of its kind in North America. Each faculty also has its own resources. Queen's houses one of the largest art galleries in Ontario and also has a smaller, student-run gallery. The phys-ed center at Queen's is a recreational/fitness facility, as well as a teaching facility for the School of Physical Education. The center features a pool, ten racquet courts, an ice hockey rink, an indoor jogging track, three weight rooms, and two dance studios. The campus also has an outdoor stadium, six playing fields, a track, and 16 tennis courts.

STUDENT HOUSING AND SERVICES

Queen's offers ten residence halls on campus, and a number of university-owned apartment rentals nearby. Students say that the halls are one big party, and although they offer a good way to meet new people, it's hard to get much work done if you live there. Residences house mainly first-year students, and vary in terms of size and facilities. Most are catered, and all come furnished with the basics (bed, desk, lamp, dresser) and phone and internet connection. Housing costs will set you back about $5,600 per year.

The university's comprehensive network of student support includes the writing center with its many tutorial programs, career services, health and counseling services, and a walk-home service, which provides students with escorts after dark (that sounds seedy, but you know what we mean).

CAMPUS LIFE

School spirit is very high at Queen's, especially where sports are concerned. A healthy rivalry has existed between the two top Canadian universities for many decades, and the school's annual "kill McGill" games are the setting for many traditions shaped by Queen's Scottish heritage—kilt-and-tam wearing and the singing of the school song, "Oll Thigh Na-Bannghinn" (Gaelic for "The College of the Queen Forever"), to the tune of "The Battle Hymn of the Republic." There are 40 varsity teams, the most of any university in North America besides Harvard. Queen's actively recruits athletes, but holds them to an unusually high academic standard. One student anonymously commented that this might be the reason that the Queen's teams aren't so hot. Nevertheless, the university boasts a number of Olympic medalists as graduates, as well as a figure skating team that has been the provincial champion for the past seven years.

Queen's Alma Mater Society is the oldest student association in Canada and sponsors some 220 student clubs and 1,000 on-campus jobs. Some faculties are known for being their own little communities, such as the Faculty of Applied Science, which has its own pub and traditions such as the annual grease pole climb and April Fools' pranks. (Engineering students have also been known to paint themselves purple for big football games.)

ADMISSIONS AND FINANCIAL INFO

Admissions at Queen's are very selective; they have to be because of the incredibly large number of applicants. (In 2003, the university received 37,000 applications for the 3,200 spots in the freshman class.)

Of all Canadian universities, Queen's allocates the most from its budget to student scholarships. Some scholarship opportunities may be available for international students. All undergraduate applications are processed by the Ontario Universities' Application Center. Consult their web site at **www.ouac.on.ca** for an application or more information. Students must also fill out a Personal Statement of Experience form, available on-line at **www.asq.queensu.ca**. Apply by February for fall entrance.

 CONTACTS

Student Recruitment and International Initiatives
Queen's University
Richardson Hall
Kingston, Ontario K7L 3N6
Canada

Continues ☞

Phone: 613-533-2218
Fax: 613-533-6754
E-mail: liaison@post.queensu.ca
URL: www.queensu.ca

Ontario Universities Application Center
170 Research Lane
Gruelph, Ontario N1G 5E2
Canada

Phone: 519-823-1940
Fax: 519-823-5232
URL: www.ouac.on.ca

Trent University

Peterborough, Ontario

AT A GLANCE

For the past ten years, Trent has consistently been listed in the top
20% of Canada's small universities by *Maclean's* magazine's annual university ranking. The college-town university prides itself on
offering small classes and a strong sense of community while providing its students with a well-rounded education in the liberal arts
and sciences.

> **Total Enrollment:** 4,500
> **Undergraduate Enrollment:** 4,063
> **Male/Female:** 33/67
> **Student/Faculty:** 22/1
> **SAT Scores:** 1100 required
> **Tuition:** $7,219 per year
> **Accreditation:** Member of the Association of Universities
> and Colleges of Canada and the Association of
> Commonwealth Universities

CAMPUS AND LOCATION

The University of Trent was founded in 1963 in the small town of Peterborough, Ontario. With its five residential academic colleges, it is one of the few universities in Canada to be built around a college system. (Students describe the colleges as being like "intimate neighborhoods in an active city.") The university's Symons campus is home to three residential colleges and Trent's main academic, sports, and research facilities. This 1,400-acre campus is situated along the banks of the Ontonabee river with its modern building nestled among forests and hills. The campus has 12 specified "nature areas" that are used for teaching and research in Trent's acclaimed environmental studies program, as well as for recreation. The other two colleges are housed in Victorian buildings in a residential area of Peterborough about 15 minutes away. A shuttle bus makes daily trips between the campuses.

Peterborough is a cozy college town of 74,000 in the Kawartha Mountains about a one-and-a-half-hour drive from Toronto, although students don't necessarily feel the need to venture far to enjoy themselves. "If you don't want to have to deal with driving, there's lots to do in town—good restaurants and movies and shows," one student told us. For more info on the town visit **www.city.peterborough.on.ca.**

ACADEMICS

Classes at Trent are generally taught through a weekly lecture and then a small weekly or biweekly seminar. Students also get a lot of one-on-one time with professors through Trent's system of resident advisors, or dons. Students feel that this helps them stay on top of their work. "If it wasn't for my don, I don't think I would have done nearly as well," one student said. Trent offers undergraduate degrees in many areas. Most students take a four-year honors degree (as opposed to the three-year general degree).

FACILITIES

Symons campus is home to the Trent library, two main computer labs, a science complex and environmental sciences center, and the main sports complex, which has a pool, racquet sport courts, a basketball court, weight and cardio rooms, and rowing facilities.

STUDENT HOUSING AND SERVICES

Trent guarantees housing to all international students and also assists students with finding off-campus apartments. Amenities vary throughout the residential colleges, but all dorms have their own laundry, dining, athletic, recreational, and academic facilities, as well as live-in dons. Students say that this greatly contributes to the closeness that they feel to their professors, and that being able to live and work in the same place is "so great, especially in the winter. You can just roll out of bed and into class!"

Trent's support services include the health center, the Trent University Emergency First Response Team (a student-run EMS unit), security telephones around campus, and a free Trent bus service around campus and into Peterborough. The academic skills center provides a number of extracurricular and credit workshops and individual tutoring to help students brush up their study techniques.

Trent's international program offers advice on issues like immigration, employment, and health insurance, and it also organizes an orientation.

CAMPUS LIFE

Since all students must choose a college to join before the start of their academic careers (even if they live off campus), the colleges become a very important part of social life at Trent. Each college organizes its own events and activities, like visiting writers, artists, and lecturers series. Outside of the colleges, though, there are many university-wide student activities, clubs, and sports teams (both varsity and intramural). Off campus, the town of Peterborough sponsors many cultural happenings, like the annual Summer Festival of Lights, which features live music, boat shows, and fireworks, and other events like the Rainbow Youth Coalition's Rainbow Dances twice a month for gay and lesbian students in the area. If you want to get away from it all, the surrounding Kawarthas Lakes region offers spectacular natural beauty and all kinds of outdoor sporting activities.

ADMISSIONS AND FINANCIAL INFO

U.S. students are required to have a 3.0 GPA for admission. Apply by June 1 for fall entry and by October 15 for spring entry. Contact the registrar's office at **liaison@trentu.ca** for an application and more info.

The Trent International Program (TIP) offers renewable full- and partial-tuition scholarships to qualifying non-Canadian students, and all students may be eligible for one-time entrance grants of $500–$2,000. Scholarships are awarded based on academic performance, extracurricular involvement, and financial need.

International students are eligible to work part-time during school and full-time over vacations.

CONTACTS

Trent International Program
Trent University
1600 West Bank Drive
Peterborough, Ontario K9J 7B8
Canada

Phone: 705-748-1314
Fax: 705-748-1624
E-mail: tip@trentu.ca
URL: www.trentu.ca

Office of the Registrar

Phone: 705-748-1215
Fax: 705-748-1629
E-mail: liaison@trentu.ca or Registrar@trentu.ca

Ontario Universities Application Center
170 Research Lane
Gruelph, Ontario N1G 5E2
Canada

Phone: 519-823-1940
Fax: 519-823-5232
URL: www.ouac.on.ca

University of British Columbia

Vancouver, British Columbia

AT A GLANCE

With fraternities, sororities, and more than 38,000 students, this may seem like your average huge state school. But UBC's student diversity, incredible scenic beauty, and academic reputation (especially strong in the sciences) make it one of the most popular universities in the area. Where better to get a degree in forestry or environmental studies than in the lush, wooded mountains and peninsulas of the Pacific Northwest? One American student summed it up when he wrote, "I picked UBC because I wanted a school that was just as good as any in the States, but gave me more bang for my buck."

Total Enrollment: 38,634
Undergraduate Enrollment: 28,030
Male/Female: 43/57
Student/Faculty: 15/1
SAT Scores: Not required
Tuition: $15,529 per year

CAMPUS AND LOCATION

In 1906 McGill University, the renowned Canadian institution, took over what was then Vancouver College, establishing the McGill University of British Columbia (MUCBC). In 1915, however, the university separated from McGill to become simply UBC, and moved to its current location on 1,000 lush acres on the western tip of the Point Grey Peninsula overlooking the Pacific Ocean, the Vancouver skyline, and the snowcapped Costal Mountains. The university's main campus, which combines gothic architecture and modern glass buildings, is painstakingly landscaped with many formal gardens and is bordered on the east by the Pacific Spirit Regional Park, a huge forest.

UBC is about 30 minutes from the heart of downtown Vancouver, which is Canada's third-largest city with a population of about two million. As one of the closest points to Asia in North America, Vancouver is known for its diverse ethnic and cultural makeup. With great museums, galleries, and a growing film and music scene, this safe and clean city is also close to the mountains and beaches that provide a plethora of outdoor activities.

UBC itself offers some of the city's finest attractions, including the Museum of Anthropology, the Chan Center for the Performing Arts, and the UBC botanical garden. The area's main (and possibly only) drawback is its dreary weather. Like most of the Pacific Northwest, winters, although generally mild in temperature, are long, dark, and drizzly. On the other hand, the constant rain makes for some of the most beautiful and lush flora in North America, which really becomes apparent in the summertime.

ACADEMICS

The University of British Columbia offers hundreds of undergraduate majors across its 12 faculties and 11 schools. The majority of students are humanities and social sciences, science, engineering, or commerce majors, but UBC is also known for its strong forestry programs. Regardless of their area of study, all first-year students must take an introductory English literature and composition class (which is reported to be pretty boring) and many majors also require students to fulfill certain requirements outside of their faculty (i.e., science students have to take humanities classes and vice versa). Class size, especially in the beginning years, is usually very large. One student said, "It is not unheard of to find yourself in lec-

The University of
British Columbia's spires overlook
the forests of the Pacific Northwest.

tures with 300 other people." But then again, classes that big are
usually broken up into smaller discussion groups run by grad students. With such a variety of academic options, registering for
classes can be a bit confusing, but each faculty has advisors to assist students with the process.

FACILITIES

Academic resources are very impressive at UBC. With 14 branches,
the university library is one of the largest research libraries in
Canada. There are also a number of applied science research facilities (which is one of the big draws for the engineers who flock to
UBC) including the Tri-University Meson Facility (TRIUMF), "one
of the world's largest national accelerator facilities for research in
subatomic physics." UBC has just recently set up a campus-wide

wireless network; by the end of 2003 students will be able to connect wirelessly to the internet across most of the campus. Other facilities include the Asian Center, the new Liu Center for Global Studies, the Museum of Anthropology, the botanical gardens, the Aquatic Center, the student recreation center, a conference center, and a sports stadium. UBC food services has tons of locations around campus, including Mini-Marts (which are open late), Subway, Japanese food, Chinese food, pizza, fast-food outlets, and even Starbucks. Each residential complex also has many of its own sports, recreational, and dining facilities. UBC is like a city unto itself, complete with theaters, shops, pubs, restaurants, art galleries, museums, and concert halls.

STUDENT HOUSING AND SERVICES

UBC offers eight campus residence complexes made up of a number of dorms. Most first-year students will be housed in Totem Park or Place Vanier, complexes designed to provide students with a sense of community otherwise lacking at the huge university. These dorms accommodate students in double or single rooms furnished with the basics and a high-speed internet connection and telephone outlet. Each hall has its own resident advisor who helps organize social activities like movies, trips, and dances. The dorms in Totem Park and Place Vanier center around the Commonsblock, which houses the cafeteria and after-hours snack bar, weight room, game room, and 24-hour front-desk staff. These dorms provide a natural way to meet people and make friends at a school so huge that one student said, "Sometimes you feel that you'll never see the same face more than once." For first-year students who are looking for somewhat less "hand holding" in the residence life, the Ritsumeikan-UBC House is an interesting option. This dorm complex puts up UBC and Japanese students from Ritsumeikan University in Kyoto in four-bedroom apartments to provide a cultural exchange. Place Vanier also offers Korea-UBC House for a similar exchange with Korea University, and UBC is currently building Tec de Monterrey–UBC House, which will bring students from UBC and Mexico's Tec de Monterrey University together.

All freshmen are required to be on the meal plan, which is very comprehensive and works at all the university's many food service locations.

UBC offers a broad range of student support services. The university has its own teaching hospital and dental school, and offers comprehensive medical and psychological counseling and a wellness center. Career services offers standard advice, and academic counseling and advising is available to students through their individual faculties. The university also provides a night walk-home service and campus bus to help students navigate the sprawling campus. Every year UBC offers an orientation program for first-year students called "Imagine." This orientation is run by student "MUG" (My Undergraduate Group) leaders. A special orientation for U.S. and international students is also held at the start of each term.

CAMPUS LIFE

Student life is varied at UBC. The student union building sponsors many guest speakers and activities, more than 220 student-run clubs, and one of the largest intramural sports programs in Canada. Frat parties are somewhat popular, and students enjoy hanging out at Pit, the campus bar. In general, however, there is not thought to be much of a sense of community outside of the individual faculties. Sporting events are not widely attended, and many students feel that the student body is made up of many commuter students. Still, the city of Vancouver offers pretty much anything one might need in the way of culture and entertainment, and the surrounding mountains, beaches, and forests make UBC popular with outdoorsy types.

ADMISSIONS AND FINANCIAL INFO

A minimum 2.6 GPA is required for acceptance at UBC. SAT or ACT scores are not required, but can be helpful; 1300 or higher on the SAT or a 27 or higher on the ACT is recommended.

Apply by March 31 for fall, although some programs that require a portfolio or audition may have earlier deadlines.

A limited number of International Leader of Tomorrow awards ranging from $10,000 to $24,000 may be available to international students depending on financial need and academic merit. UBC also offers scholarships for the following sports: men's baseball, basketball, crew, cross-country running, men's football, golf, ice hockey, rugby, soccer, swimming, track and field, volleyball, and women's field hockey.

 CONTACTS

International Student Recruitment and Reception
University of British Columbia
Room 1206—1874 East Mall
Vancouver, British Columbia V6T 1Z1
Canada

Phone: 604-822-8999
Toll-free: 877-292-1422
Fax: 604-822-9888
E-mail: international.reception@ubc.ca
URL: www.ubc.ca

University of Toronto

Toronto, Ontario

AT A GLANCE

The University of Toronto is one of the largest universities in North America. Students flock here for its vast resources, the quality and breadth of the academic programs (especially the faculties of Engineering and Arts and Sciences), and its cosmopolitan location in downtown Toronto. Because of its size, U of T is definitely not known for its community spirit, but some of its notable alumni include author Margaret Atwood, entrepreneur Jeff Skoll (creater of eBay), actor Donald Sutherland, filmmakers David Cronenberg and Norman Jewison, and many Canadian political figures.

Total Enrollment: 63,109; 11% North American, 24% European, 13% Middle Eastern/African, 32% Asian
Undergraduate Enrollment: 51,223
Male/Female: 44/56
SAT Scores: 1200 required; 1300 required for Applied Science faculties
Tuition: $10,661 per year

CAMPUS AND LOCATION

The University of Toronto was founded in 1827 by a British Royal Charter and is the largest university in Canada. The Royal Ontario Museum, Pollution Probe, Canadian Opera Company, the Toronto Symphony, and the Royal Conservatory of Music were all started at U of T.

The university's main campus, St. George, is spread out in downtown Toronto near Chinatown in an area with cute cafés, restaurants, and tons of vintage stores. Toronto is a wonderful city, comparable to New York or London in the scope of its shopping, dining, nightlife, cultural environment, and subway system, but it's got the added bonus of also being incredibly safe and clean.

ACADEMICS

U of T offers undergraduate degrees across four main faculties: Applied Sciences and Engineering, Music, Physical Education and

Health, and Arts and Sciences (the most popular). Academics are competitive across all courses. Classes tend to be very large, especially freshman year, but they get smaller as the years go up, and are often broken up into tutorial groups with teaching assistants. U of T offers a co-op program known as the Professional Experience Year, or PEY. This 12- to 16-month work program, mainly for students in engineering or computer sciences, is designed to give students a practical component to their studies and a competitive edge in the job market. The university boasts many achievements in scientific research, including the development of the first pacemaker, and (on the macabre side) it is the only university in the world to have an academic chair dedicated to suicide research.

FACILITIES

The university library holds over 12.8 million volumes and is one of the top research libraries in North America, second only to Harvard and Yale. The Hart House, U of T's all-purpose student-run auditorium/recreational complex, is home to a bank, a bookstore (check out **www.uoftbookstore.com**), live music venues, dining facilities, and the Justina M. Barnicke Art Gallery. Despite its extensive facilities, students complain that campus access to the internet is "disappointingly limited."

STUDENT HOUSING AND SERVICES

All first-year students are guaranteed a place on campus, and living in one of U of T's nine residential colleges is considered to be an important part of the freshman year experience. At such a huge university, many students feel that it is the only way to feel part of a community. As one student who lived off campus put it, "I'd rather have experienced life on campus because it would have been closer to everything and friendlier."

Support services are comprehensive at U of T. They include a health and psychiatric clinic, a chaplain's association, housing service, a legal aid service, a career center, and an international student center, as well as academic support and classes at the Advice on Writing Center.

CAMPUS LIFE

There is not much school spirit at U of T. Many students are just in it for the education, making themselves scarce after class ends. Although each college and faculty organizes many of its own social events, students report that these "factions" sometimes discourage mingling within the college. "Probably the best way to meet people outside of your college is to join a club," said one student. At U of T there are certainly enough student clubs to suit any interest, such as camera, film, chess, diplomacy, debates, bridge, table tennis, orchestra, jazz ensemble, chorus and singers, music, and yoga. Check out the student newspaper, *The Varsity,* on-line at **www.thevarsity.ca**.

Off campus, students find plenty of ways to amuse themselves in Toronto. Bloor Street, with its many cafés and bars, is right across from the university's main building and is a popular destination for students. The huge city is made incredibly accessible by its great public transportation system. (Check out *eye,* a local weekly arts and events on-line magazine, to see what's going on in town this week at **www.eye.net**.)

ADMISSIONS AND FINANCIAL INFO

Admissions at U of T are fairly competitive. The university operates on an academic year rather than on a semester or quarter system. Apply by February 1 for the faculties of Applied Science and Engineering, Music, and Nursing and by March 1 for all other faculties.

U of T is recognized as a postsecondary institution for Federal Stafford Loans. For information about alternative loans, e-mail Admissions and Awards at **osap@adm.utoronto.ca** and be sure to include your mailing address.

CONTACTS

Admissions and Awards
University of Toronto
315 Bloor Street West
Toronto, Ontario M5S 1A3
Canada

Phone: 416-978-2190
Fax: 416-978-7022
E-mail: ask@adm.utoronto.ca
URL: www.utoronto.ca or www.myfuture.utoronto.ca

CHINA

University of Hong Kong

Hong Kong, China

AT A GLANCE

Founded in 1911 by the Chinese government, the University of Hong Kong, or HKU, is the one of the oldest and most prominent universities in China. Its large and modern campus incorporates ten faculties, and the university is especially known for its science programs.

> **Total Enrollment:** 14,800
> **Undergraduate Enrollment:** 9,100; 700 international
> **Male/Female:** 47/53
> **SAT Scores:** 1100 required
> **Tuition:** $5,500 per year

CAMPUS AND LOCATION

The main campus is located on the northwestern slopes of Hong Kong Island, a beautiful area overlooking the vast Victoria Harbour. Hong Kong is a subtropical city of about 3.5 million situated on the southeastern coastline of China, facing the South China Sea.

The two official languages of the city are Cantonese and English, and as a testament to its long years of colonial rule, there are really two very distinct Hong Kong experiences—Chinese and British. A friend of ours from Hong Kong who attended a British school there grew up without ever learning any Chinese.

Hong Kong Island is the epicenter of government, commerce, and fancy shopping. Hong Kong's most traditional "Chinatown" is located here, as are some famous areas like Wan Chai, a colorful harbor district once famous for "carousing sailors," which now offers many clubs and cultural activities. Causeway Bay is a popular shopping and dining neighborhood, as is Aberdeen, an ancient fishing port on Hong Kong Island's South Side. The beaches of Repulse Bay and Deep Water Bay offer a scenic escape from a huge city that can be somewhat overwhelming.

ACADEMICS

Academics are serious at HKU. Students choose from 47 undergraduate degree subjects across the university's ten faculties: Art, Architecture, Business and Economics, Dentistry, Education, Engineering, Law, Medicine, Science, and Social Sciences. Students take about 80% of their credits in courses in their major area of study, and the rest are focused on Chinese language, information technology, general studies, and electives. First-year classes often involve large lectures of up to 100 people, accompanied by smaller tutorials. The school year is divided into two 18-week semesters—15 weeks of classes and three weeks of exams. The China VacTrain Program offers students an opportunity to participate in two-month internships with companies in mainland China, and the HKU Worldwide Undergraduate Student Exchange Program organizes study abroad exchanges with over 100 overseas universities.

FACILITIES

Students agree that one of the best aspects of HKU is its facilities. The university library's six branches house over two million volumes, and a vast network connects computer labs and dorm rooms to its on-line databases. Several student centers offer restaurants, theaters, darkrooms, and dance studios. The student union in the Hsu Long Sing Amenities Center has meeting rooms, a computer lab, a campus store, and a copy center. Sports facilities include two indoor sports centers—the Flora Ho and Lindsey Ride Sports Centers—which are situated close to the main campus on Pokfulam Road. Each has a large gym, an outdoor swimming pool, and fitness and weight-training rooms. Another sports complex, the Stanley Ho Sports Center at Sandy Bay, includes an athletics stadium with a synthetic running track, an Olympic-size swimming pool, three grass sports pitches, a floodlit artificial turf pitch, golf driving bays, and a softball diamond. Altogether, the sports center manages a total of 17 tennis courts in four locations.

STUDENT HOUSING AND SERVICES

The university currently has a total of 3,092 residential places in ten halls with a variety of facilities. The residence halls are reported to be very social places, and many organize their own sports teams and extracurricular activities.

HKU offers comprehensive health care with free primary and dental care, as well as preventive services such as a wellness clinic, a well woman clinic, a hepatitis B clinic, and immunizations. The personal development and counseling center helps students with academic and personal issues, and the careers education and placement center helps place students with employers and runs job and résumé skill workshops.

CAMPUS LIFE

All undergraduates are required to join the student union, the core of extracurricular student activity. At the beginning of their first year, the union holds an orientation program designed to introduce students to its many activities and clubs. The union puts out two publications (in Chinese), the *Undergrad* and *Campus Bi-Weekly*,

A view of the University of
Hong Kong's Eliot Hall

and produces TV shows by Campus TV. Each hall and faculty also
has its own student association.

ADMISSIONS AND FINANCIAL INFO

Students with American high school credentials must have a senior-
year GPA of 2.0 and two AP tests with scores of 3 or higher for acceptance at HKU. Apply by February 28 for fall admission. For
information on international scholarship opportunities, contact the
academic services enquiry office.

CONTACTS

Academic Services Enquiry Office
Room UG05
Knowles Building
University of Hong Kong
Pokfulum Road
Hong Kong
China

Phone: 852-285-92433/78634
Fax: 852-254-01405
E-mail: afss@reg.hku.hk
URL: www.hku.hk

COSTA RICA

University of Costa Rica, Rain Forest Adventure
San Jose, Costa Rica

AT A GLANCE

The Costa Rica Rain Forest Adventure may sound more like a ride at Disneyland than an academic program, but it offers students the unique chance to study rain forest conservation in one of the most ecologically varied spots in the world. Students must have at least one semester of college under their belts to participate in this semester program.

> **Total Enrollment:** 15
> **Tuition:** $8,000 per semester
> **Accreditation:** Students receive credits directly through the University of Costa Rica

CAMPUS AND LOCATION

The Rain Forest Adventure program is based at the University of Costa Rica in San Jose, the cultural center of Costa Rica, but since so much class time is spent in the field, one might say that the tropical forests are really the campus. Costa Rica is a small peninsula in Central America, between Nicaragua and Panama, with the Pacific Ocean to its west and Caribbean Sea to the east. Costa Rica is only about 41,000 square miles, but it holds around 4% of the world's biodiversity. It also has some of the most varied tropical ecosystems in the world, including cloud forests, lowland rain forests, mangroves, and paramos.

ACADEMICS

Students take three classes a semester—Tropical Ecology, Costa Rican Natural History, and Biodiversity and Conservation—as well as Spanish language classes. All classes are taught in English (except Spanish, obviously) by professors at the University of Costa Rica's School of Biology.

The program also emphasizes field training, and students take many supervised excursions in small groups of four to five students into the rain forests. Students learn how to collect and analyze data, write scientific papers, and present oral reports. Although only American students participate in the program, it is actually listed in the University of Costa Rica's course catalog, and the credits earned are from the university. Each transcript comes with an English translation and a grade conversion chart.

FACILITIES

Students have access to all of the University of Costa Rica's facilities, which are pretty standard for a large science-oriented institution: computer labs, a Spanish-language library focused on tropical ecology, a cafeteria, and a gym. The Rain Forest Program also has its own small resource library (in English) and its own field equipment. Students in the program have access to exclusive field sites—the San Ramon Forest Reserve, one of the best field sites in Costa Rica and one of the only cloud forests free of tourists, as well as the Volcan Cacao Biological Station and Cerro de la Muerte Biological Station.

STUDENT HOUSING AND SERVICES

Students live with carefully screened families in the San Jose area. Each homestay offers a private room, breakfast, dinner, and laundry facilities. Most host families do speak English, but students are encouraged to communicate in Spanish. Students have access to the infirmary at the University of Costa Rica and are also covered under the center's comprehensive health insurance.

CAMPUS LIFE

The central location of San Jose allows students to easily travel around Central America and the Caribbean. The center arranges many four-day weekends to encourage traveling and allocates $2,000 from each student's tuition to cover the cost of group trips around the area.

ADMISSIONS AND FINANCIAL INFO

Applicants must have completed at least one college-level natural science class (biology, ecology, natural history, etc.) and have a GPA of at least 2.5 to be considered for the program. Students must also show a serious interest in ecology.

 CONTACTS

World Class Adventures in Education
17812 SH 16 S
Pipe Creek, TX 78063

Phone: 800-321-7625
E-mail: info@educationabroad.com
URL: www.study-abroad-costa-rica.com

CZECH REPUBLIC

Anglo-American Institute for Liberal Studies

Prague, Czech Republic

AT A GLANCE

The Anglo-American Institute for Liberal Studies is a small semi-accredited college in a vibrant and historically student-friendly town. Although students may take courses in a number of areas, AAILS offers only two accredited degree programs—Humanitics and Business Administration, the more popular of the two.

Undergraduate Enrollment: 315; 60% Czech
Male/Female: 45/55
Student/Faculty: 7/1
SAT Scores: 950 required
Tuition: $1,840 per semester
Accreditation: Czech Ministry of Education, European Council of Business Education

CAMPUS AND LOCATION

The Anglo-American Institute for Liberal Studies is spread out over two locations in the city of Prague. AAILS's main Lazenska campus is located in a restored eighteenth-century building, formerly the palace of the knights of Malta. The building is situated at the foot of the Charles Bridge in the Mala Strana, one of Prague's six famous historic neighborhoods. Buildings dating as far back as the tenth century A.D. house more modern amenities, like Bohemia Bagel, Prague's first bagel café. The college library and other recreational facilities are about 35 minutes away in AAILS's Na Jetelce building in Prague's Vysocany district.

The early '90s were a time of great change and growth for the newly formed Czech Republic. Prague saw a great resurgence in tourism and is now a major hot spot for European and American backpackers, students, and general fun-seekers. The city is home to a growing underground film and arts community, and its club and music scene rivals those of Berlin and London. The city is also reported to have many terrific jazz venues. For more information, visit **www.pragueonline.cz.**

ACADEMICS

The college offers a number of interdisciplinary undergraduate degree programs from its schools of Business Administration, Social Sciences and Humanities, and Legal Studies. Full-time students take four or five classes per semester (for 12 to 15 credits). In order to graduate, all students must also take eight general college courses. These courses, which are usually completed during a student's first two years, cover the bases of a well-rounded liberal arts education and include classes in the humanities, economics, and law, as well as practical subjects like composition and computer skills. AAILS offers a four-year degree option to Business Administration majors whereby they can complete their fourth year at Central Michigan University and earn an American degree.

FACILITIES

The Na Jetelce building (named after the street it's on) houses AAILS's main academic and recreational facilities. The college library has over 14,000 holdings and is one of the largest collections of English-language books in the Czech Republic. A computer lab and sports facilities are also located in the building. There are no dining facilities at either campus, but there are many restaurants and cafés near the main campus.

STUDENT HOUSING AND SERVICES

The college doesn't have its own housing facilities, but it will help students get special rates at a Czech dorm just outside of Prague. The student services office can set students up in hotels or hostels or with roommates in city apartments.

The small student services office can also help students find English-speaking personal counselors, doctors, and specialists when needed.

CAMPUS LIFE

Students report that at AAILS the student body is "serious and focused, but able to have fun." The student council throws parties throughout the year at "cool places with cheap drinks and good DJs." The student council also organizes student clubs and other activities—it is currently in the process of introducing extracurricular foreign language classes to AAILS. The student newspaper, *At The Lennon Wall,* is run by the journalism program. You can read it on-line at **www.atthewall.cjb.nct**. Off campus, students report that local hot spots El Centro and Bombay Café are especially popular with AAILS students.

ADMISSIONS AND FINANCIAL INFO

AAILS accepts applications on a rolling basis. Applications for the fall semester should be received by May 31, but late applications will be considered on a case-by-case basis until the end of August. Applications for the spring semester are due by November 15, but late applications will be accepted until mid-January. Students must submit an application form, a high school diploma, and standardized test scores.

All full-time students with GPAs of at least 2.5 may be eligible to apply for need-based scholarships of up to 25% off their total tuition. Some competitive merit-based scholarships may be available to students with a 3.5 GPA. A limited number of on-campus work-study jobs are also available.

 CONTACTS

Anglo-American Institute for Liberal Studies
Lazenska 4
118 00 Praha 1
Prague
Czech Republic

Phone: 420-257-530-202
Fax: 420-257-532-911
E-mail: info@aac.edu
URL: www.aac.edu

EGYPT

American University in Cairo

Cairo, Egypt

AT A GLANCE

An American school in the Arab world that caters primarily to a Middle Eastern student body, AUC offers a strong American liberal arts education, including one of the world's most comprehensive Middle East and Egypt studies programs taught in English.

Undergraduate Enrollment: 4,236; 201 American
Male/Female: 60/40
Average Class Size: 15
SAT Scores: 1000 required
Tuition: $11,250 per year
Accreditation: The Commission on Higher Education of the Middle States Association of Colleges and Schools, incorporated in the state of Delaware

---

CAMPUS AND LOCATION

American missionaries founded the American University in Cairo in 1919 with the goal of benefiting Egyptian cultural and intellectual life and presenting Americans with a better understanding of the often-misunderstood region. Years later, the university has grown into a substantial research and teaching faculty with a well-respected press. AUC, which follows an American liberal arts teaching tradition, has a primarily Egyptian student body and a conservative attitude. One student recommended that before arrival at AUC, students should read as much as possible about culture, contemporary history, and politics in the Arab world.

The main building of AUC is housed in the turn-of-the-century Moorish palace on Tahrir Square in downtown Cairo. The whole campus takes up five city blocks near the Egyptian museum, the National Cultural Center, and government buildings.

Cairo is both a historical and thoroughly cosmopolitan city. (Arabic is the official language, but most locals also speak English.) Students love the city for all of its cultural offerings, but many had negative comments about the level of pollution. One student said, "Cairo is a great city, but it is large, crowded, noisy, and dirty. It is the third world. On the other hand, it is a city full of culture and history. It is vibrant and alive. It is truly a city that never sleeps. The people are also very friendly and welcoming." Students also enjoy the fact that the city is very cheap, making it much easier to indulge in shopping and traveling than in the States. Women, however, should be cautious when traveling on their own. One student said, "One of the worst things for me is the way men treat women they see in the street. Walking down the street in downtown Cairo is an exercise in self-control and endurance. For a Western woman, especially a very white and thus very conspicuous woman, it can become a trial of necessity, though I never felt directly in danger of being attacked. Most of it is supposedly harmless." Another female student advised women to carry pepper spray and if possible to travel at night with a group of guy friends. For a good tourist web site visit **www.egyptvoyager.com**.

ACADEMICS

The academic mission of AUC is to provide students with a broad education, emphasizing Middle Eastern studies. To this aim, the university offers Bachelor of Arts and Bachelor of Science degrees in a wide variety of subjects in the schools of Business Economics and Communication, Humanities and Social Sciences, and Sciences and Engineering. All students are required to take a core curriculum in traditional liberal arts classes, as well as learn to read and write in Arabic. Small classes foster student-professor relationships, and in many instances, assignment deadlines are very liberal. Students report that academics tend to be pretty relaxed and some visiting students felt that that they were not expected to work as hard as their degree-seeking peers. These study abroad students also remarked that if academics had been harder, they would not have had nearly as much time to enjoy the city of Cairo, which is a valuable learning experience in itself.

AUC's Arabic Language Institute offers intensive (not for credit) language courses three times a year. These programs attract about 100 visiting students who are encouraged to integrate into the rest of the student body.

FACILITIES

The multilingual main library, academic computing services, and Apple multimedia lab are housed in a large, modern, glass building with a courtyard that is a hub of student daytime activity. A nearby turn-of-the-century villa houses AUC's Rare Books and Special Collections library, which includes artifacts and materials on the Middle East and Egyptology and Islamic art and architecture, as well as the personal collection of renowned Egyptian architect Hassan Fathy.

HOUSING AND STUDENT SERVICES

Students rave about the dorms at AUC, which are located a 15-minute shuttle ride (provided free by the college) away on the island of Zamalek. Residence life reflects the conservative attitudes of the Middle East. An AUC representative said, "In the Middle East, there is very much an expectation for women to be under the protection of their families. In the case of these women who have

American University in Cairo's President Gate
displays the university's Moorish architecture.

left home to pursue their education, the college is expected to take over in the role of the protector." Men and women are totally prohibited from contact with each other in any living areas of the dorm. Students do not seem to really mind this, and hanging out in the residences' separate recreational areas is a popular coed pastime. Facilities at the residence include a TV lounge, dining hall, bookstore, exercise room, and outdoor garden. Each shared room has central a/c, phone, internet access, and available maid and laundry services. Students remark on how much more spacious and clean the rooms are than in American dorms, and said that the residence felt more like a hotel then a college dorm. The dorms house mainly international students because most Egyptians live with their families until graduation. Students say that to really experience being immersed in an Egyptian experience, you should live in an apartment off campus. Rentals are fairly cheap and easy to come by and can be arranged through a student services office.

The main sentiment among American students at AUC is that "the ISSO (International Student Support Office) is wonderful." Students get the support they need, whether it be help in mailing a letter or getting a visa. AUC also serves its students and alumni comprehensively in the area of employment counseling. Career Advising and Placement Services (CAPS) offers a career resources library, a job shadowing program, summer internship programs, career objective assistance, and it helps students set up relationships with area employers through an employment fair twice a year. (Says AUC: "CAPS maintains equal opportunity compliance and follows affirmative action principles.") Other services include a full-time basic health care clinic, with a part-time office in the residence hall, and psychological counseling.

CAMPUS LIFE

American students at AUC feel that they are pretty well integrated into the primarily Egyptian student body, but it does take effort because of the differences in culture and language. Foreign women at AUC usually have it a little easier than their male peers, simply because they have access to a much bigger dating pool. (Middle Eastern women are generally off limits to American men.) One former American student said that she had a boyfriend within a week of arriving in Cairo. Another American student remarked that she felt that in general is was difficult to make friends with Egyptian women because they "seemed to accept all of the common stereotypes about American women (including but not limited to promiscuity, arrogance, etc.), and thus didn't generally want to have much to do with us."

The office of student housing sponsors many cultural and recreational activities and trips throughout the year, and international and Egyptian students interact with each other in the student union and its numerous clubs. AUC also offers extracurricular art and music activities such as the choral group, the music group, the arts group, and the Egyptian folk dance group. These groups regularly compete and perform, as does the AUC theater company, one of the most active student groups on campus. It is open to all interested students.

Off campus, the city of Cairo offers students endless distractions from their studies. "There's always something to do or a place to go, a tourist attraction to wander through or a camel to ride." AUC students populate the many western bars and cafés around the city such as Harris Cafe, a coffeehouse open 24/7, even during Ramadan (which students say is very important, because it is hard to find food when the whole country is fasting). Cafe Tabasco is a fairly good pizza place, and the Sand Bar is "a great American-style bar popular with AUC students."

ADMISSIONS AND FINANCIAL INFO

Admissions are highly competitive—each fall, about 2,500 students compete for 700 places in the freshman class. AUC offers an Academic Achievement Scholarship program whereby students in the top 25% of new students will receive $4,000 per year off tuition, while students in the second 25% will receive $1,000 off. For more information on other merit- and need-based scholarships, contact the admissions office.

CONTACTS

American University in Cairo
Office of Enrollment Services
113 Kasr El Aini Street
P.O. Box 2511
11511 Cairo
Egypt

Phone: 20-2-797-5012
Fax: 20-2-794-4728
E-mail: enrolauc@aucegypt.edu
URL: www.aucegypt.edu

U.S. Office

American University in Cairo
420 Fifth Avenue, Third floor
New York, NY 10018-2729

Phone: 212-730-8800
Fax: 212-730-1600
E-mail: aucegypt@aucnyo.edu

FRANCE

American University of Paris

Paris, France

AT A GLANCE

The American University of Paris is one of the most popular American universities overseas, especially for students interested in art history and international affairs. It is the only American liberal arts college in one of the most vibrant and beautiful cities in the world, and you don't have to speak a word of French to go here.

> **Undergraduate Enrollment:** 800; 38% E.U., 35% American
> **Male/Female:** 64/36
> **Student/Faculty:** 15/1
> **SAT Scores:** Required, but no minimum
> **Tuition:** $20,516 per year
> **Accreditation:** The Commission on Higher Education of the
>   Middle States Association of Colleges and Schools,
>   incorporated in the State of Delaware

CAMPUS AND LOCATION

In 2001, the American University of Paris (AUP) celebrated its fortieth year as an American liberal arts school in Paris. The campus is located in Paris's chichi 7th Arrondissement (near the Eiffel Tower and Trocadero), a very expensive and beautiful but slightly stuffy part of town. It is, however, very convenient since the Champs-Elysées is close by and offers many 24-hour cafés, late-night shopping, and big blockbuster movie theaters. If you love movies, art, cigarettes, and croque monsieur this is absolutely the city for you. For more information, visit **www.thingstodo-paris.com**.

ACADEMICS

Students describe classes at AUP as being "competitive and intense. The professors push students to the limit, expecting them to be prepared, participate, and be active in class." One student mentioned "in a semester you may often find yourself with five 10- to 20-page papers and it can get a bit hectic." On the other hand, a fair number of students claimed that the draw of AUP is the experience of living in Paris, and not necessarily the education. In any case, the university offers degrees across 12 areas. In keeping with the liberal arts tradition, students must also fulfill a general education requirement. These include two courses in English writing and French, two courses in the humanities, and two courses in lab science. AUP also offers a unique set of courses for entering students called the first bridge program. All freshmen must participate in these interdisciplinary classes that meet twice a week. The program aims to encourage discussion and teamwork and to acclimate high school students to college work. Once a week, the 20-member class breaks in half to form two discussion groups called Reflective Seminars. The RS professor becomes the students' academic advisor and helps them plan next year's academic program.

Internship programs are required for all communications, computer science, and international finance majors, but all full-time degree-seeking students with a 3.0 average and French proficiency are also eligible to apply for an internship.

FACILITIES

AUP has five computer labs with over 90 PCs and Macs, as well as a special lab for teaching and research in quantitative sciences.

Other facilities include an American Express–sponsored student-run café. AUP doesn't have its own sporting facilities, but the sports association leases athletic facilities around Paris for student use and has a special rate with Gymnasse fitness clubs.

STUDENT HOUSING AND SERVICES

AUP houses students temporarily upon arrival in Paris in the FIAP, an upscale international hostel (Mariah actually stayed there briefly on an NYU program and says that it's pretty comfortable, as hostels go). Since AUP doesn't have its own dorms, a housing advisor helps students find their own accommodations, usually in a "chambre de bonne"—a small studio with a bathroom down the hall—or a room in a French household.

AUP does not have its own health services, but it offers students a health insurance plan and can make arrangements with English- and French-speaking doctors, dentists, psychiatrists, and specialists. Other services include an office of career development, which assists students in résumé development and finds internships and summer employment for students.

CAMPUS LIFE

One of the students' favorite aspects of AUP is the sense of community among the small and "energetic" international student body. For a small school, AUP also has quite a number of student clubs like art4U, a choir, the feminist coalition, film and fine arts clubs, a Christian club, a music club (which has its own rehearsal space and recording studio), a queer club, and a theater group. The student senate gives funding to new clubs in September of each year, so starting your own is always a possibility. Student publications include a yearbook, a student newspaper, a business journal, a humanities journal, and a creative writing journal. The Amex Cafe, a student-run bar on the AUP campus, is a very popular spot, especially during its Thursday evening happy hour. Students report that the frequent parties hosted by the student government associations are also popular.

ADMISSIONS AND FINANCIAL INFO

AUP operates on a rolling admissions policy. Financial aid is offered based on need and academic merit, and students seeking this
option should apply as early as possible. The American Association
of Teachers of French offers full AUP freshman-year tuition to ten
winners of its annual Grand Concours French contest. (For more
info, talk to your French teacher, or visit **www.frenchteachers.org**.)
U.S. students are not eligible to work in France, but the Office of
Student Affairs posts some listings for odd jobs.

 CONTACTS

American University of Paris
Admissions Office
6 Rue de Colonel Combes
75007, Paris
France

Phone: 33-1-40-6207-20
Fax: 33-1-47-0534-32
E-mail: admissions@aup.edu
URL: www.aup.fr

_____

U.S. Office

American University of Paris
950 South Cherry Street, Suite 210
Denver, CO 80246

Phone: 303-757-6333
Fax: 303-757-6444
E-mail: usoffice@aup.edu

Parsons School of Design, Paris

Paris, France

AT A GLANCE

Parsons Paris is a tiny art school associated with the prestigious Parsons School of Design in New York City. It is also the only art school in Europe to offer a four-year American Bachelor of Fine Arts degree. This four-year program is offered to Fine Arts majors only. All other students take only two years of their programs at the Paris campus.

Undergraduate Enrollment: 165; 45% American
SAT Scores: Required, but no minimum
Tuition: $18,417 per year
Accreditation: National Association of Schools of Art and Design (NASAD), Middle States Association of Colleges and Schools

CAMPUS AND LOCATION

Parsons Paris was founded in 1920 as the Paris ateliers for Parsons New York. The campus has since moved locations a number of times before finding its permanent home in two adjacent town houses near the Eiffel Tower in the 15th Arrondissement.

ACADEMICS

Because classes are so small, Parsons Paris students have the advantage of being able to take many field trips and get lots of individual attention from their professors. In their first year, students take foundation classes only, designed to introduce them to the many different aspects of visual and liberal arts and to prepare them for their subsequent years of specialized study. These foundation courses emphasize drawing, seen by the college as the "fundamental visual language common to all art and design fields." Students may also take classes in French literature, culture, and language.

In their second year, students choose their major from Fine Arts, Communication Design, Fashion, Illustration, Photography, or Design and Management, the one program leading to a Bachelor of Business Administration degree.

FACILITIES

The campus's facilities include painting, drawing, and sculpture studios, a large multimedia computer lab, a student gallery and fashion ateliers, printmaking facilities, and a newly renovated photo lab. There are no residence, dining, or athletic facilities.

STUDENT HOUSING AND SERVICES

The student services office pretty much does it all. It helps students find off-campus housing, provides referrals for English-speaking health and counseling services, assists students with all French administration issues, and organizes school social events. Parsons Paris also offers a very comprehensive medical insurance plan.

CAMPUS LIFE

Parsons Paris students are a dedicated bunch. They come to Paris to pursue their art and explore the city, and not necessarily to get involved in extracurricular activities. Most time on campus is spent in the studios, and while there is officially a student government, its contributions vary from year to year depending upon the interest level of the current student body.

ADMISSIONS AND FINANCIAL INFO

Admission is highly selective. Applicants are reviewed based on academic records as well as the art and design skills represented in their portfolios. For scholarship information, contact the admissions office.

 CONTACTS

Parsons School of Design, Paris
14 rue Letellier
75015 Paris
France

Phone: 33-1-45-7739-66
Fax: 33-1-45-7710-44
E-mail: admissions@parsons-paris.com
URL: www.parsons-paris.com

Schiller International University, Paris Campus

Paris, France

AT A GLANCE

Schiller International University is a small American university based in Florida with campuses around the world, offering programs in International Business, International Relations, and Hospitality. Students can take all four years at any one of its campuses, but it's also possible to be a true international jet-setter and spend each semester at a different campus. Students come to the Schiller Paris campus for its romantic Left Bank location and for the strong International Business programs.

> **Total Enrollment:** 120; 20 American
> **Undergraduate Enrollment:** 70
> **Male/Female:** 55/45
> **Student/Faculty:** 10/1
> **Tuition:** $7,879 per semester
> **Accreditation:** Accrediting Council for Independent
>   Colleges and Schools (ACICS)

CAMPUS AND LOCATION

SIU's Paris campus is located near Montparnasse on the left bank of the Seine. The university's main building is within walking distance of many monuments and the Latin Quarter, which is not, as Mariah embarrassingly enough once thought, named for a Latin American population, but because as far back as the fourteenth century, the neighborhood was home to the University of Paris, where students spoke in Latin. The Latin Quarter is now a famous hub of student activity, with wonderful cafés, bars, bookstores, and independent movie theaters.

ACADEMICS

SIU Paris offers a Bachelor of Business Administration with specializations in International Business and Marketing, and a B.A. in International Relations and Diplomacy with a specialization in Interdepartmental Studies. The campus also offers Associate degrees in International Relations and General Studies.

Students in both degree programs must complete requirements in some subjects other than their concentration, and must also reach an intermediate level of French.

FACILITIES

The small campus building houses the Schiller library and a small PC computer lab. SIU Paris pays for students' membership to the American Library, a large private English-language library.

STUDENT HOUSING AND SERVICES

There is no on-campus housing, but the SIU staff places students in private or shared apartments. The campus offers support services through its job placement office, undergraduate academic advisors, and a dean of students for counseling and advice.

CAMPUS LIFE

SIU Paris and the student council organize social and cultural activities and trips throughout the semester, including Fourth of July, Bastille Day, and Chinese New Year parties, as well as Thanksgiving dinner and many special student "ethnic" dinners. The student council can arrange discounted prices for theater and movie tickets and other cultural activities.

ADMISSIONS AND FINANCIAL INFO

Students apply directly to the Schiller Florida campus. The university has a rolling admissions policy, so there is no application deadline, but students going to overseas campuses are suggested to apply at least two months before the beginning of the semester because of visa complications.

SIU participates in many Federal Aid programs, as well as a number of Florida State Aid programs like the Bright Future Scholarship and the Florida State Assistance Grant. SIU also offers a variety of scholarships and grants based on academic merit and financial need. For more information, e-mail **Financial_aid@schiller.edu**.

For information on Schiller's other locations, see Schiller Heidelberg (page 136), Schiller Leysin (page 233), and Schiller Madrid (page 225).

 CONTACTS

Schiller International University Paris Campus
32, Boulevard Vaugirard
F-75015 Paris
France

Phone: 33-1-4538-5601
Fax: 33-1-4538-5430
E-mail: info-schiller@schillerparis.com
URL: www.schillerparis.com

Continues ☞

U.S. Campus

Schiller International University
Florida Admissions Office and Central
  Administration Offices
453 Edgewater Drive
Dunedin, FL 34698-7532

Phone: 727-736-5082
Toll-free: 800-336-4133
Fax: 727-734-0359
E-mail: admissions@schiller.edu
URL: www.schiller.edu

GERMANY

International University of Bremen

Bremen, Germany

AT A GLANCE

An exciting and very young scientific research–oriented university with brand-new facilities, involved professors, and a study abroad exchange with Rice University in Texas, IUB offers more than your average small international university.

> **Undergraduate Enrollment:** 330 (growing significantly each year)
> **Male/Female:** 53/47
> **Student/Faculty:** 6/1
> **SAT Scores:** 1300 average
> **Tuition:** $16,090 per year
> **Accreditation:** Through the German government

CAMPUS AND LOCATION

Founded in 1999, the International University of Bremen may be young, but what it lacks in experience it makes up for in vitality. A 75-acre parklike campus holds the first two of three projected res-

One of the International University
of Bremen's many academic buildings

idential colleges. The third college, as well as a campus center containing conference and event facilities and the information resource center, are slated to be completed by the end of 2003. Over the next few years, more buildings for teaching and research will be built.

The modern campus is located in a suburb of Bremen, near the Weser and Lesum rivers. Bremen is a 1,200-year-old harbor city in northern Germany. It is relatively small (with a population of half a million) and safe, yet cosmopolitan, and known for its tolerance and multiculturalism. It is home to many art galleries and theaters as well as restaurants, bars, clubs, and live music venues as well as the Beck's Brewery.

ACADEMICS

Academics at IUB are research-oriented. The professors, many of whom are young professionals with the air of excited visionaries, reflect this hands-on approach. In fact, students say that one of the best things about IUB is the ability to form close relationships with their instructors. Students and faculty interact on a personal level in class and on campus where students and professors share living quarters.

The university offers a three-year Bachelor of Arts or Bachelor of Science degree program in two schools: Engineering and Science, and Humanities and Social Sciences. A required transdisciplinary program makes students take classes outside of their majors. However, unlike a traditional set core curriculum program, students at IUB meet with their academic advisors to hand-pick electives and create their own set of courses. Academics can be very demanding—one student told us that he spent about 75 hours a week in class and doing homework. Students are expected to take 120 credits in three years, as well as to complete an internship the summer between their second and third year. IUB has a partnership with Rice University in Texas, and encourages student and faculty exchanges between the two institutions.

FACILITIES

Students say that one of the best things about the college being so young is that the facilities are modern and sparkling. Amenities include a central lab building and several integrated labs, an information resource center (which is a futuristic library), two sports halls, a gym, a cinema, and a student center building.

STUDENT HOUSING AND SERVICES

All undergraduates live on campus in residences with single bedrooms done up in a hip Ikea minimalist style. Each residential college has a faculty member who lives in the residence with his or her spouse as the college masters. They organize activities and events in the college and act as advisors. The colleges also have their own dining halls, game and TV rooms, lounges, study areas, and meeting rooms.

In subsequent years, IUB will be adding more student services, but as of now, the university offers professional personal counseling, career services, and a student service center, staffed with IUB volunteers available for all sorts of student questions and needs. An interfaith house sponsors many kinds of religious services.

CAMPUS LIFE

The small size and residential nature of IUB makes for an involved student body who feel a strong sense of community on campus. Student clubs run the gamut from football to classical dance to wine tasting, as well as a student radio station and newspaper. Because the university is so young, all student groups are recently founded, and new students report that they don't feel intimidated about getting involved, or even starting up their own clubs.

ADMISSIONS AND FINANCIAL INFO

Admission to IUB is highly selective and need-blind. Students are admitted based on academic achievement, but the administration emphasizes that it is equally important for candidates to demonstrate strong leadership skills, the ability to think creatively, and an interest in world affairs. Admission operates in four rounds—December, February, April, and June. Apply early to improve your chances of acceptance and of receiving financial aid. IUB offers work-study programs, low-interest loans, and some merit- and need-based scholarships.

 CONTACTS

Postal Address

International University of Bremen
P.O. Box 750 561
D-28725 Bremen
Germany

Continues ☞

Visitors' Address

International University
Postfach 750561
D-28725 Bremen
Germany

Phone: 49-421-200-4200
Fax: 49-421-200-4113
E-mail: admission@iu-bremen.de
URL: www.iu-bremen.de

International University in Germany

Bruchsal, Germany

AT A GLANCE

A selective and small university in a very small town, IUG's goal is to train international business managers through its strong Information and Communication Technology, International Management, and Cultural Studies programs. The university's corporate outreach programs and relationships with international companies help to ensure that its small student body will find jobs after graduation.

Total Enrollment: 240; 50% international
Undergraduate Enrollment: 80
Male/Female: 65/35
Student/Faculty: 8/1
SAT Scores: Required, but no minimum
Tuition: $10,720 per year
Accreditation/Affiliation: by the State of Baden-Württemberg;
   Associate member European Council of Schools (ECIS)

CAMPUS AND LOCATION

The International University in Germany was founded in 1998 in the small town of Bruchsal, an area of Germany known for its rolling hills and many lakes. The area's natural beauty, including its proximity to the Black Forest, makes it a must to get involved in outdoor sports. Bruschal itself is home to a famous eighteenth-century baroque palace, and a number of other cultural attractions, bars, and restaurants, but on the weekends, students usually head to the larger nearby towns of Heidelberg, Stuttgart, and Strasbourg. Students find that Bruchsal is perfectly located for traveling throughout Europe, especially to Switzerland, Austria, Italy, and France.

ACADEMICS

IUG comprises two schools: the School of International Technology and the School of Business Administration. It also offers a small science and liberal arts program, but this is not the university's strongest academic area. Information technology is prominent in all aspects of education at the university, and students are required to be computer literate. Students must also have their own computer in order to fulfill certain IT requirements. Students in all departments must participate in an internship and must take German classes in preparation. IUB also has exchange arrangements with a number of universities around the world, and students are encouraged to study abroad for at least one trimester.

FACILITIES

IUG has a small but generally adequate campus library, and more extensive computer labs. The newly renovated "swimming and leisure center" offers indoor and outdoor facilities, along with a gym and fitness room. The student cafeteria is open 24 hours a day, and there is a student-run mensa café, which is open only for lunch.

STUDENT HOUSING AND SERVICES

Dorms at IUG are very cushy. Students are put up in three-bedroom apartments with shared kitchen and bathroom facilities and a phone. Almost all rooms have balconies, which students say are big enough to accommodate impromptu parties. Each residence building has its own laundry facilities in the basement. Housing costs are between $200 and $450 per month, which covers utilities, internet access, and cable TV.

The university offers a career services office that places students in internships and jobs and helps with their résumés and interview skills. There is also a writing lab to help students with papers, but this service is primarily used by students who aren't fluent in English.

CAMPUS LIFE

IUG offers a number of organized activities throughout the year, including weekly student-faculty social events. Sports are also popular, and the university organizes a number of athletics clubs.

Bruschal, although small, does have a few hot spots—Barrocko and Brazil are two popular local bars—but to really get down, students usually head to Stuttgart, which has a better club scene.

ADMISSIONS AND FINANCIAL INFO

Apply by June 30 for fall entry. Some need- and merit-based financial aid of up to 20% of the annual tuition may be available to qualified American students. The university can also administer student loans.

CONTACTS

International University in Germany
D-76646 Bruchsal
Germany

Phone: 49-7251-7000
Fax: 49-7251-700-150
E-mail: info@i-u.edu
URL: www.i-u.de

Schiller International University, Heidelberg Campus

Heidelberg, Germany

AT A GLANCE

The Heidelberg campus has been around for almost 40 years, making it SIU's oldest overseas campus. Located in a small university town, it specializes in business degrees. (For more details on SIU in general, see Schiller International University, Paris Campus, page 125.)

Total Enrollment: 200; 30% American
Undergraduate Enrollment: 140
SAT Scores: Not required
Tuition: $6,592 per semester
Accreditation: Accrediting Council for Independent
  Colleges and Schools (ACICS)

CAMPUS AND LOCATION

The small Heidelberg campus (consisting of administrative offices, a library, a computer facility, classrooms, and two wings of dormitory rooms) is housed in a landmarked Art Nouveau villa at the edge of a forest, about 20 minutes from the center of Old Heidelberg. The Collegium Palatinum, a German-language school closely affiliated with Schiller, and the German-American Institute, which sponsors many lectures, films, and cultural events, are just across the road. Located in the valley of the Neckar River between wooded mountains and the Rhine plain, Heidelberg is not short on scenic beauty. It's also a pretty happening town. The presence of the University of Heidelberg, Germany's oldest university, lends the would-be sleepy town an air of vitality and culture—there is always something going on and students everywhere. Heidelberg also has NATO and U.S. Army bases, which add to its international atmosphere.

ACADEMICS

SIU Heidelberg offers Bachelor of Business Administration degrees with concentrations in International Business, Management, Marketing and Information Technology, and Bachelor of Arts degrees with concentrations in International Relations and Diplomacy, International Economics, and Interdepartmental Studies. Associate degrees are available in General Studies and International Business. Degree programs are made up of courses in the major and electives slightly outside of the major. Students are generally required to reach an intermediate level in a foreign language.

FACILITIES

SIU has two computer labs and a small campus library. Students also have access to libraries of the German-American Institute and the University of Heidelberg. An on-campus bookstore sells semester reading requirements and other sundries. The campus doesn't have its own sports facilities, but all SIU students are offered free membership to the Institute for Sport and Sport Sciences at the University of Heidelberg.

STUDENT HOUSING AND SERVICES

The word used most often to describe student accommodations at the Heidelberg campus is "sparse." Neither this, nor the fact that the majority of students in residences seem to have a problem with cleaning up after themselves, affect the popularity of the residence halls. Students describe living on campus as an incredible experience, allowing them to really bond with people of all nationalities and backgrounds. Students also enjoy the convenience and low cost of living on campus, and the fact that the university residence staff is always on hand for help and advice. For students who want to live off campus, a list of local apartments is available, and homestays can be arranged through the university.

SIU Heidelberg offers limited support services, mainly through its admissions faculty, who can refer students to English-speaking doctors in the area, but it does have a number of organized career days, with visits from company recruiters.

CAMPUS LIFE

SIU Heidelberg organizes many educational, cultural, and social trips and events, like tours around Germany, ski trips, and a canoe trip to Strasbourg. Off campus, students say that the Untere Neckarstrasse is a good local strip with lots of bars and restaurants, but most Schiller students prefer to frequent clubs in town or in nearby Frankfurt. Students enjoy weekend exploring and can buy a discounted Semester Ticket from SIU, which is good for travel on all buses, trams, and trains in the Heidelberg area and Rhein-Neckar region.

ADMISSIONS AND FINANCIAL INFO

See Schiller International University Paris, page 127.

CONTACTS

Heidelberg Campus
Schiller International University
Bergstrasse 106
69124 Heidelberg
Germany

Phone: 49-6221-45810
Fax: 49-6221-402703
E-mail: 100520.611@compuserve.com
URL: www.siu-heidelberg.de

U.S. Campus

Schiller International University
Florida Admissions Office and Central
  Administration Offices
453 Edgewater Drive
Dunedin, FL 34698-7532

Phone: 727-736-5082
Toll-free: 800-336-4133
Fax: 727-734-0359
E-mail: admissions@schiller.edu
URL: www.schiller.edu

GREECE

American College of Greece, Deree College
Athens, Greece

AT A GLANCE

American College of Greece's Deree College is a traditional American undergraduate college in a suburban setting, considered by Greek standards to be one of the best universities in the area. Students come here for the strong marketing program and for the lowest tuition prices of any American university overseas.

> **Undergraduate Enrollment:** 6,837
> **Male/Female:** 35/65
> **Student/Faculty:** 27/1
> **SAT Scores:** 900 required
> **Tuition:** $2,517 per semester
> **Accreditation:** The New England Association of Schools and Colleges

CAMPUS AND LOCATION

Founded in 1923, the American College of Greece is the oldest and largest American college in Europe. ACG consists of Pierce College, a high school; Junior College, a two-year college offering associate degrees; and Deree College, a four-year liberal arts college made up of two campuses—Aghia Paraskevi campus and the downtown campus established in 1971.

The Aghia Paraskevi campus is located about six miles from the center of Athens on a modern 65-acre property on the western side of Mount Hemettus. Aghia Paraskevi is known for its marketplace, old mansions, and the Festival of the Bull, which the town has celebrated since 1774. The area is full of monuments and historical sites, like the ruins of the ancient Aeolian temple of Napaios Apollo in nearby Klopedi and the remains of a third-century B.C. Ionian temple. The town is only a short drive from downtown Athens, a bustling cosmopolitan city that offers students plenty in the way of nightlife, great shopping, restaurants, and cafés. The majority of full-time undergraduates study at the Aghia Paraskevi campus, while the downtown campus in Athens is geared mainly toward professionals pursuing business training.

ACADEMICS

Deree College's School of Arts and Sciences and School of Business Administration offer B.S. and B.A. degrees in many areas of study. In most degree programs students must fulfill a general education requirement. These courses include Composition 1 and 2, Literature and Composition, Public Speaking, and Ethics. Students must also complete classes in the arts, humanities, social sciences, and math, depending on their major. On the administrative end of their academic careers, students report that registration can sometimes be a big hassle, and they advise undergraduates to fulfill their major requirements as soon as they can so as not to get "stuck" at ACG forever.

FACILITIES

In 1997, the Deree library had three extra stories tacked onto it, and it was also fully computerized. Some students feel that the college should have beefed up its computer labs, too—only about 100 computers are available on campus for general use. The Aghia Paraskevi campus also has fancy athletic facilities like an outdoor heated Olympic-sized pool and a two-story gym, tennis courts, a track, and the first AstroTurf sports field in Greece. The communications building with its black-box theater, TV studio, and open air theater, which recalls the traditions of ancient Greece, provides an outlet for the performing arts on campus.

HOUSING AND STUDENT SERVICES

ACG does not offer any on-campus housing, but the international office helps overseas students find apartments and homestays with Greek families in Athens and the neighboring suburbs.

The college offers health care and personal and academic counseling, and the center for career services provides current students with a broad range of counseling, workshops, and job placement services, as well as a career resource library. The student SERF (Safety, Emergency, Rescue, and Fire) team is trained to assist in emergency situations and provides a walk-home service to students at night. New students start the year off with an orientation program designed to introduce them to the campus and to their peers with tours and social events.

CAMPUS LIFE

Because of its reasonable price and generous financial aid packages, the student body at ACG is representative of a wide group of Greek society (i.e., not just a bunch of aristocratic émigrés). Because there are no dorms and the campus is in an urban environment, ACG is not big on what we'd call "school spirit." But there is still an active student union (that students enroll in for a fee) and a student council. There are also many curricular societies (academic clubs) organized by major. These work in conjunction with a course curriculum to offer lectures and special seminars. The office of student affairs organizes cultural and recreational clubs that only accept students in good academic standing. There are also a number of intercollegiate and intramural sports teams and recreational athletic clubs. Throughout the year, ACG organizes student trips around Athens and Greece to the many cultural and historical sites.

ADMISSIONS AND FINANCIAL INFO

There are no stated academic requirements for admission to ACG, although the average GPA of its student body is 3.0. Apply by July 10 for fall entry or January 10 for spring entry, but students are advised to apply as early as possible. An interview with an ACG representative is required. Representatives are stationed all over the world; contact the admissions office to find one in your area.

Students with a GPA of at least 2.7 may be eligible for yearlong financial aid. ACG also offers reduced fees for siblings, regardless of financial need.

 CONTACTS

Mr. Nick Jiavaras, Director of Enrollment Management
American College of Greece
Deree College Admissions Office
6 Gravias Street
GR—153 42 Aghia Paraskevi
Athens
Greece

Phone: 30-1-0600-9800
Fax: 30-1-0600-9811
E-mail: dereeadm@hol.gr
URL: www.acg.edu

Continues ☞

American College of Greece
Deree College Admissions Office
Downtown Campus
6–8 Xenias Street
GR—115 28
Athens
Greece

Phone: 010-748-6580
Fax: 010-748-3463
E-mail: dereeadm@acg.edu

American College of Thessaloniki

Thessaloniki, Greece

AT A GLANCE

This college offers strong business management programs and is located in a beautiful Mediterranean seaside town that offers students all the natural beauty and rich history of Greece without all the annoying European tourists. The college has recently added a degree in Hotel and Restaurant management to its curriculum.

Undergraduate Enrollment: 750; 25% international
Male/Female: 53/46
Student/Faculty: 10/1
Average Class Size: 18
SAT Scores: 1000 required
Tuition: $11,250 per year
Accreditation: The New England Association of Schools and Colleges Commission on Institutions of Higher Education

CAMPUS AND LOCATION

The American College of Thessaloniki was founded in 1980 as a division of Anatolia College, one of Greece's oldest secondary schools. It operated as a two-year American-style liberal arts associate degree program until 1990, when it expanded to include a four-year bachelor's degree program in the arts and sciences, and it is still expanding; the college recently acquired land next to its current wooded campus for the site of an independent campus for undergraduate studies. It built its first building on this site in 1995, and many of the university's new facilities are located here. Thessaloniki was founded in 315 B.C. and is the second-largest city in Greece. The ancient sea town is home to many temples, monuments, and museums, but also many modern amenities, trendy restaurants, bars, and clubs. The layout of the city reflects both the historic and the modern with wide concrete avenues and also small winding cobblestone streets and tucked-away gardens going back thousands of years. The ACT campus is near several beaches, and students can enjoy sailing, camping, hiking, and exploring the surrounding islands and coves. The Chalkidiki peninsula, one of the most popular seaside resort areas in Greece, is only an hour's drive away.

ACADEMICS

ACT offers B.A. or B.S. degrees in nine subjects, most notably Business, History, English, and Foreign Affairs, with a variety of concentrations. The college has recently added a hospitality concentration to its list of business programs. The college also offers certificate programs in bilingual translation, film subtitling, and Cisco networking. ACT hosts a study abroad program for visiting college juniors and a special summer theater program.

Because of the college's small size, classes are intimate, teaching is extremely personalized, and students develop a strong rapport with their professors. Students at ACT respond well to this kind of teaching; nearly 40% of each graduating class goes on to pursue postgraduate degrees in the U.K. or the U.S. All students must take a core curriculum comprised of classes in the humanities, social sciences, math and computer sciences, and natural sciences.

FACILITIES

The Bissell Library was opened on ACT's new campus site in 2002, and provides up-to-date computer reference materials, databases, periodicals, and a bilingual collection. The campus's main building houses the majority of classrooms, administrative and faculty offices, two computer labs, the college bookstore, and the cafeteria. Athletic facilities include a gym, soccer fields, and tennis courts.

STUDENT HOUSING AND SERVICES

ACT doesn't offer much in the way of student housing, so most students prefer to be placed off campus by the housing office in apartments or in dorms at Greek universities in the area. In this popular setup, international students really get a chance to mingle with their Greek peers. Most housing is located near shopping areas with restaurants and decent public transportation.

Services at the small campus are somewhat limited. The ACT counseling center provides emotional and academic support. Professional counselors lead workshops and also something called "drama therapy." Health care services can be arranged through the office of student affairs.

CAMPUS LIFE

The ACT student body is an especially involved one. The college holds a club fair at the beginning of every year to introduce students to more than 15 academic and recreational clubs, including yearbook and newspaper. The college also organizes events like a Mardi Gras carnival, lectures, community services activities, leadership skills workshops, and intramural sports.

ADMISSIONS AND FINANCIAL INFO

Apply by November 30 for fall admission. Each year ACT offers two full four-year scholarships through the John and Mary Pappajohn Foundation. This grant is open to students with a high school diploma who are interested in studying Business Administration or Computer Management Information Systems.

 CONTACTS

Ms. Roula Lebetli
Director of Admissions
American College of Thessaloniki
P.O. Box 21021
555 10 Plea
Thessaloniki
Greece

Phone: 30-2310-398-238
Fax: 30-2310-301-076
E-mail: rleb@act.edu
URL: www.anatolia.edu.gr/act

College Year in Athens

Athens, Greece

AT A GLANCE

College Year in Athens was established in 1962 in association with the International Center for Hellenic and Mediterranean Studies. It offers summer, semester, and yearlong programs in ancient and modern Greek culture and civilization to college sophomores, juniors, and seniors. It is one of the best-established study abroad centers in Southern Europe.

Enrollment: 100
Male/Female: 40/60
Average Class Size: 15
Tuition: $10,800 per semester; $20,000 per year (includes room and board)
Accreditation: Incorporated in Delaware

CAMPUS AND LOCATION

College Year in Athens's modern four-story center consists of an auditorium, student lounge, classrooms, administrative offices, computer lab, library, and roof garden. It is located in downtown Athens in one of the city's fanciest neighborhoods near the Olympic stadium of 1896. The area is, needless to say, very safe and clean, home to many cafés, upscale stores like Gucci, and a "Eurotrashy" population.

ACADEMICS

Classes at the CYA center are offered in two academic fields: Ancient Greek Civilization and Eastern Mediterranean studies. These two reading- and writing-intensive courses are organized into three levels for beginning to advanced students, and both fields offer classes in Modern Greek language. Students generally take four courses a semester, but if their home university requires that more credit be earned, a fifth course may be taken at the center for no extra charge. As with many study abroad programs, a common problem at CYA is that students from all levels are in class together, and this tends to slow things down. One student reported that academics were pretty lax, but then added that this was great, because it allowed for more time to travel and explore the area. However, another student noted that he loved his anthropology class, and that he learned a "surprising amount of Greek." Throughout the semester, students take many field trips with the whole group, and also in smaller groups on class-specific trips. Courses are assessed throughout the semester by written assignments and at the end in final exams.

FACILITIES

Facilities at CYA are reported to be somewhat meager. One student told us that the only good thing about them was the cable TV in the student lounge. CYA's small library contains materials pertaining to ancient, modern, and medieval Greece and the Mediterranean. Students also have access to the British Council Library, the National Library, and other English-language libraries in the area.

STUDENT HOUSING AND SERVICES

Students live with other American students in program-owned apartments in the Kolonaki/Dexameni/Maraslio area of Athens, about a 20-minute walk away from the CYA center. The chichi neighborhood at the bottom of a wooded hill is near many small shops and a weekly outdoor produce market. Each student apartment has two to three double bedrooms with a common area, kitchen, bathroom, and balcony. The apartments are fully furnished and come with a connected mobile phone to be kept in the common area for emergencies. (After the orientation period, students usually get their own mobile phones.) On Monday through Saturday, one meal a day is provided in the campus dining room, which is located between the apartments and the main center. Yearlong students have the option to apply for a limited number of places in homestays their second semester.

CYA has a special arrangement with a nearby private hospital, which allows students to be admitted immediately in emergencies. Otherwise, local English-speaking doctors are available for lesser catastrophes. Students are required to come to Greece with their own health insurance. An orientation program is organized at the beginning of each semester, during which students are broken up into groups of eight and assigned to an advisor known as a big brother or sister.

CAMPUS LIFE

On such a small campus, students report that your social life is really what you make it. Each year though, students organize a number of extracurricular activities like group trips, drama productions, and sports. Athens also offers a hopping bar and club scene. Cafe 48, a nearby American-theme bar, is apparently so popular with CYA students that the Greek owners offer them drink specials. CYA's program seems to be popular with Greek-American students, who offer an enormous social advantage to their peers. Said one non-Greek student, "I got to meet lots of Greek kids through my American friends who spoke Greek fluently and had family in Athens."

ADMISSIONS AND FINANCIAL INFO

For admission to the program, students are generally required to have a 2.7 GPA for admission, and have two years of college under their belts. They must also have CYA's Statement of Study Abroad Approval signed by their home university. See the web site for more details.

 CONTACTS

College Year in Athens
P.O. Box 390890
Cambridge, MA 02139

Phone: 617-868-8200
Fax: 617-868-8207
E-mail: info@cyathens.org
URL: www.cyathens.org

GRENADA

St. George's University

Grenada, West Indies

AT A GLANCE

Located on a lush tropical island in the West Indies, St. George's was founded in 1976 as a private medical school, and due to its international success, has recently expanded to include a school of veterinary medicine and a small undergraduate school of arts and sciences that offers Bachelor of Science degrees with a liberal arts component.

Total Enrollment: 2,370; 71% Caribbean
Undergraduate Enrollment: 154
Male/Female: 58/96
Student/Faculty: 5/1
SAT Scores: Not required
Tuition: $14,500 per year
Accreditation: Member of Association of Caribbean Tertiary Institutions

CAMPUS AND LOCATION

The School of Arts and Sciences is housed on St. George's University's beautiful Grand Anse campus on the island of Grenada. This newly renovated sprawling $30 million campus used to be a beach resort and is conveniently located near five grocery stores, an open-air produce market, and the local airport. (In fact, it's so close that some students have complained that the sound of airplanes thundering overhead disturbs the otherwise peaceful campus.) Grenada's climate is truly tropical, a consistent 85 degrees, with only two main seasons—wet and dry. For more about the island, check out **www.grenadagrenadines.com**.

ACADEMICS

The School of Arts and Sciences offers only two undergraduate degree programs: a B.S.in Medical and Life Sciences and a B.S. in International Business with an emphasis in Administration or Accounting. The school also offers a premedical and a preveterinary program, which are three-year nondegree programs, designed as preparation for the School of Medicine or the School of Veterinary Medicine. Premed and prevet students can make special arrangements to complete requirements leading to the B.S. in Medical and Life Sciences. Students in all programs must fulfill a certain number of general education requirements. These include classes in Math, English, Speech, Humanities and the Arts, Social and Behavioral Sciences, and Natural Sciences.

FACILITIES

St. George's Grenada campus has recently expanded to include brand-new, state-of-the-art labs (the school administrators boast that the gross anatomy lab features "ample cadavers") and a new electronically equipped Founder's Library with a number of computer labs and study rooms. In addition to its regular holdings, the Founder's Library also houses the Institute of Caribbean Studies' archive collection and the Ovid full-text Core Biomedical Collections Database.

There are three restaurants and snack bars located around campus, as well as a comprehensive fitness center.

St. George's clock tower on
the beautiful island of Grenada

STUDENT HOUSING AND SERVICES

All freshmen must live on campus in undergraduate dorms their
first year. These three-story air-conditioned buildings accommodate students in suites of six single rooms with shared bathroom
and kitchen facilities.

Support services at St. George's are comprehensive. Academic support is offered through the Dean of Students' Office and the Department of Educational Services. The DES provides review courses, time management seminars, study skills development, and faculty development. Professional and peer counseling services are also available. University health services offers a student health clinic on campus and has use of the facilities at Grenada General Hospital for emergencies. The wellness center is a separate clinic, which focuses on holistic health and offers medical and dietary review, fitness evaluations, and classes in stress reduction.

CAMPUS LIFE

St. George's student government association is a very active group that organizes a wide variety of student clubs and activities. SGU's athletic program is also popular, and grows with every term. Currently, the campus has intramural programs for basketball, volleyball, soccer, flag football, badminton, tennis, street hockey, and a developing softball and cricket tournament, as well as several St. George's Rep teams that take part in community competitions.

Students at St. George's tend to be locally minded, and the university's volunteer services organization gives students a chance to get involved in the Grenada community. St. George's also gives back to the community through the Shell-sponsored Shell Cricket Academy, an on-campus training facility to cultivate young West Indian cricket players.

ADMISSIONS AND FINANCIAL INFO

American students should apply through the North American Correspondence office. Contact the office for more details. St. George's School of Arts and Sciences does not offer any undergraduate scholarships.

CONTACTS

U.S. Office

Bob Ryan
Assistant Dean of Enrollment Planning
St. George's University
c/o The North American Correspondent
University Services, Ltd.
One East Main Street
Bay Shore, NY 11706-8399

Phone: 631-665-8500
Toll-free: 800-899-6337 x280
Fax: 631-665-5590
E-mail: sguinfo@sgu.edu
URL: www.sgu.edu

HUNGARY

McDaniel College Budapest

Budapest, Hungary

AT A GLANCE

At this two-year overseas campus of an American university, students can choose to continue their degrees at the small, private McDaniel University home campus in Westminster, Maryland, or transfer elsewhere.

Undergraduate Enrollment: 60
Male/Female: 51/49
Student/Faculty: 5/1
Average Class Size: 12–15
SAT Scores: 1000 required
Tuition: $6,900 per year
Accreditation: The Commission on Higher Education of the Middle States Association of Colleges and Schools

CAMPUS AND LOCATION

McDaniel University (formerly the University of Western Maryland until a student poll revealed that the name sounded too much like a state school) established its Budapest campus in 1995 in cooperation with College International Budapest. The campus and its facilities are housed in a beautiful nineteenth-century three-story building, formerly a Jewish high school, within walking distance of the East End Railway Station. Budapest, a city of two million, is situated on both sides of the river Duna (Danube). Eight bridges link the historic Buda on the river's west bank to the cosmopolitan business district of Pest on the east. After the end of socialism in 1989, Budapest has once again become a thriving Central European capital, and is the center of Hungarian cultural, economic, and political life with 11 universities, two opera and ballet theaters, and many museums, art galleries, and parks. Hungarian is the official language of the city, but English and German are also spoken in most tourist areas. The public transportation system includes subways, buses, and trolleys, and it is efficient and inexpensive (a monthly student pass is about eight dollars). For more on what's going on in town, visit the *Budapest Sun,* Hungary's only English-language newspaper, on-line at **www.budapestsun.com**.

ACADEMICS

McDaniel Budapest offers majors in Business Administration, Economics, Political Science, and Communications, as well as a large variety of liberal arts subjects. Students interested in focusing on subjects not available at the Budapest campus may use their two years to focus on completing the basic liberal arts requirements needed to graduate from McDaniel. A number of renowned semester study abroad programs are offered, such as Budapest Semester in History (BSH), focusing on central European history with a Jewish theme, and Budapest Semester in Mathematics (BSM).

FACILITIES

McDaniel's main Budapest center houses lecture halls, classrooms and offices, two large computer labs, a reading room, and a cafeteria. Students have access to facilities at the much larger Hungarian public university next door to the center, as well as a nearby English-language library.

STUDENT HOUSING AND SERVICES

The campus does not offer any student accommodations, but the student services office can set students up in area apartments or in local homestays. Housing and food costs are estimated at $4,000 to $5,500 per year.

At the tiny campus, the student services office acts as the only support resource. It organizes 24-hour health care through local English-speaking doctors and any other type of counseling students might need.

CAMPUS LIFE

Although very small, the student body at McDaniels Budapest is an incredibly diverse group—American and Canadian exchange and study abroad students mingle with students from around the world taking English-language university prep programs. The student union publishes a monthly newspaper and organizes many student activities like theater evenings, museum visits, evenings with guest speakers, career nights, and extracurricular programs like a video production workshop and a tango workshop. Students organize sports teams (basketball and soccer are the most popular), and each semester, trips are planned throughout the area.

ADMISSIONS AND FINANCIAL INFO

Students apply directly to the Budapest campus by June 30 for the fall semester and December 31 for the spring. Some merit scholarships may be awarded through the Maryland campus to students with high GPAs.

CONTACTS

McDaniel College Budapest
H-1406 Budapest 76
P.O. Box 51
Hungary

Phone: 36-1-413-3025
Fax: 36-1-413-3030
E-mail: admissio@mcdaniel.hu
URL: www.wmcbp-ci.hu

U.S. Office

McDaniel College Maryland
Dean of Admissions
2 College Hill
Westminster, MD 21157-4390

Phone: 410-848-7000
Fax: 410-857-2757
E-mail: admission@mcdaniel.edu
URL: www.mcdaniel.edu

ISRAEL

Hebrew University of Jerusalem, Rothberg International School

Jerusalem, Israel

AT A GLANCE

Hebrew University of Jerusalem's Rothberg International School (RIS) offers a number of flexible programs for American students. High school seniors should consider its freshman-year prep program (Mechina) designed to ease them into the rest of the student body at HUJ. Older students can look into their gap year and college semester and yearlong programs. All this in one of the most exciting and beloved cities in the world.

Total Enrollment: 24,000 (Hebrew University)
Undergraduate Enrollment: 1,000 (Rothberg International School)
SAT Scores: 1100 for Mechina; varies according to faculty
Tuition: $7,900 per year
Accreditation: Israeli Ministry of Education

CAMPUS AND LOCATION

Hebrew University of Jerusalem (HUJ) has been offering study abroad programs for international students since 1955. The Rothberg International School is housed in a state-of-the-art building on HUJ's Mount Scopus campus, near the Frank Sinatra Student Center. (Yes, "Old Blue Eyes" was a benefactor.) The university is centrally located in the 3,000-year-old city of Jerusalem, both a holy place and a thriving cosmopolitan city with a European feel, at least compared to the rest of the Middle East. Students unanimously loved the city. Said one, "Jerusalem is an amazing city with so many different cultures, languages, and traditions. The people are welcoming, the food is delicious, and there is always something going on." All that, plus the Egged bus system offers a convenient way to get around (except during Shabbat, during which there are no public buses). For a guide to the city in English, visit **www.jerusalem.muni.il/english**.

The Hebrew University has a 24-hour security network, with Israeli Defense Forces reserve guards located at all campus entrances and units patrolling the campus and the vicinity. Security has been tremendously increased since an incident in 2002, when a bomb went off in Mount Scopus cafeteria, killing nine people—the only incident of its kind in the university's 75 years. Not one American overseas student returned home in response to the attack, and in fact, it seemed to boost students' attachment to Jerusalem and to the university. One student told us, "Because of this experience I started a program for students of Hebrew University's year abroad programs to attend courses to become medics and volunteer on Israeli ambulances."

ACADEMICS

The freshman year program, or Mechina, is designed for American students to gain proficiency in Hebrew and meet the requirements needed for regular study at HUJ or at other Israeli universities. Students in this program will earn the equivalent of the Israeli Bagrut qualification. A large portion of the first semester of the Mechina is devoted to Modern Hebrew language programs called Ulpanim (or Ulpan). Before the start of the Mechina, all students must take the summer Ulpan program held during July and August through the university's Hebrew Language Department in the Faculty of Humanities. The rest of the Mechina Program is designed so that students can move into different areas of the university after freshman year, and offers three options, or "trends": the Mathematics and Exact Sciences Trend, the Advanced Economics and Social Sciences Trend, and the Humanities and Social Sciences Trend. Students in all trends must take Jewish and Israeli Studies, Calculus, and at least one introductory course. Across all trends, classes are small and intimate, and involve frequent field trips. Students mentioned that they are given a lot of freedom in their classes. One wrote that the professors don't check up on students' progress, but "they assign a lot of reading and assume that it is being done."

FACILITIES

RIS's newly built main Boyar Building has its own small computer lab and library with relevant materials. Students also have access to all of HUJ's regular facilities, including the many sports facilities such as the Cosell Center for Physical Education Leisure and Health Promotion, the Montor Outdoor Recreation Center, the Weider Physical Fitness Club, and the aerobics institute.

STUDENT HOUSING AND SERVICES

For the most part, students in the Mechina program are housed with other RIS students, unless they specifically request an Israeli roommate. Each dorm has its own madrichim, a staff of live-in Israeli students. There is no meal plan, but most residences have kitchen facilities and are near cafeterias and supermarkets.

RIS's office of student activities is set up to ensure that visiting students don't get lost in the shuffle of the larger HUJ. Students also have access to HUJ's two comprehensive health clinics, each of which has a pharmacy, lab services, a primary care physician, a gynecologist, and other specialist care. Dental care is also available at one of the clinics.

CAMPUS LIFE

The RIS office of student activities organizes extracurricular activities and clubs for its small international student body, such as hiking, tae kwon do, a photo club, and an a cappella choir, to name a few. There are also some activities designed to integrate visiting students with their Israeli peers, but RIS students report that these methods don't seem to work "unless you speak Hebrew well enough to seem like another Israeli." Another student wrote, "I barely know any Israelis from the university except those I live with in the dorm."

Off campus, students spend their time exploring Jerusalem's endless cultural, historical, and entertainment possibilities, or they take advantage of the two months off in between semesters to travel. For students looking to pursue religious interests, the office of student activities organizes religious activities for overseas students such as Home Hospitality, which gives students the opportunity to spend Shabbat and holidays with families in Jerusalem and around Israel. HUJ's Boyar Building sponsors a weekly informal religious advising event with Conservative, Orthodox, and Reform Judaism representatives and the Student Christian Forum. The Hecht Synagogue on Mount Scopus holds daily services and is the hub of the university's religious life. Christian students are also represented at the university through the Student Christian Forum.

ADMISSIONS AND FINANCIAL INFO

American students apply through the New York office. Dates are subject to change: Apply by April for fall entry and by November for spring. Some need-based grants may be available to U.S. citizens. Applications for scholarships can be downloaded from the web site; contact the New York office for more details.

CONTACTS

Office of Academic Affairs (OAA)
Hebrew University of Jerusalem
11 East 69th Street
New York, NY 10021

Phone: 212-472-2288
Toll-free: 800-404-8622
Fax: 212-517-4548
E-mail: hebrewu@hebrewu.com
URL: http://overseas.huji.ac.il

ITALY

American University of Rome
Rome, Italy

AT A GLANCE

The American University of Rome is one of the most popular American universities overseas, possibly due more to its historic and cosmopolitan setting than to its not-so-strenuous academics (although the university is reported to have a very good art history program). AUR's student body is primarily American with a large number of visiting students, but its curriculum emphasizes internationalism and is taught by university professors from diverse international backgrounds.

Undergraduate Enrollment: 440; 300 American, 66 Italian, 74 other nationalities
Male/Female: 28/72
Student/Faculty: 7/1
SAT Scores: 1000 average
Tuition: $5,570 per semester
Accreditation: Accrediting Council for Independent Colleges and Schools (ACICS)

CAMPUS AND LOCATION

The American University of Rome was founded in 1969 and is the oldest American university in the city. AUR's small campus is housed in a nineteenth-century villa on top of Rome's highest hill, the Janiculum, in a fancy residential neighborhood. It is located near Via Aurelia Antica, an ancient Roman road, and Villa Pamphili and Villa Sciarra, two of the biggest parks in Rome. The center of town is only a 20-minute bus ride away, but the neighborhood around the campus has lots of cafés, restaurants, and a large outdoor market. For an on-line guide to the city visit **www.gotoroma.com.**

ACADEMICS

AUR offers an education that combines elements of a liberal arts program with professional studies. When asked about academics, one student commented, "The academics are geared to prepare us for the working world." Some visiting American students felt that they were not learning as much in the classroom as they would be at their home institutions, while other full-time students felt that the university was not as involved as it should be with its students' academic welfare. Still, classes at AUR are small and intimate, and students are assigned an academic advisor at the beginning of the year.

The university offers Bachelor of Arts degrees in Communication, International Relations, Italian Studies, and Interdisciplinary Studies, and a Bachelor of Science degree in Business Administration. Associate degrees are offered in Liberal Arts and International Business. In addition to courses required to fulfill their majors, students must also take electives in the humanities, social sciences, and math/natural sciences. All new and transfer students are also required to take the CUNY (City University of New York) proficiency test for English and math placement. Students normally take five courses a semester, and 120 credits are needed to graduate. In-

The American University of
Rome's main campus villa

ternships for credit may be available for qualified students. Some participating companies include Fendi, Amnesty International, Associated Press, and American Express. AUR also offers a special exchange with City University of New York College of Staten Island whereby students can complete the second half of their education in Staten Island and receive a CUNY degree.

FACILITIES

AUR has its own small library on campus, which houses mainly books and articles relevant to course assignments. The university is also part of an interlibrary loan system with all of the English-language libraries in Rome, including the American Academy of Rome right next door. Campus facilities also include two computer labs, a painting and printmaking studio, a darkroom, and a multi-media lab with digital video and editing equipment.

STUDENT HOUSING AND SERVICES

AUR does not have its own dorms, but it helps students find apartments through local agents. Apartments in central Rome are generally small and expensive with bad closet space, but these drawbacks are made up for by the convenience factor of living so close to the campus (and being in such an amazing city). Students generally live in groups of three or four, but there is also a residence-style housing option, in which students live in studio apartments in a nearby hotel. Housing costs are about $5,220 per year, but vary according to accommodation.

AUR offers support services in the way of cultural and academic orientation, a writing assistance center for homework help, a study abroad and employment placement office, and professional psychological counseling.

CAMPUS LIFE

The AUR Student Government is relatively active and organizes yearlong sports and recreational activities for its small student body. There are also a few student societies, the most popular being the International Business Club, the International Liberal Arts Club, and the Drama Club. Off campus, there are more ways for students to amuse themselves in the city of Rome—culturally, historically, and party-wise. Students mentioned that nearby bar Grotta Pinta is a favorite AUR hangout.

ADMISSIONS AND FINANCIAL INFO

A 2.5 GPA is required for acceptance, but students with lower academic credentials may be considered if they show enough ability and promise. After the first semester, students in good academic standing may be eligible for university grants and work-study jobs.

A limited number of scholarships are available through the National Italian American Foundation. For more information on this particular scholarship, contact:

ITALY

Dr. Maria Lombardi, Education Director
National Italian American Foundation
1860 19th Street NW
Washington, D.C. 20009
Phone: 202-387-0600
Fax: 202-387-0800

For other scholarship opportunities, contact AUR's U.S. office.

 CONTACTS

American University of Rome
Via Pietro Roselli, 4
Rome 00153
Italy

Phone: 39-065-833-0919
Fax: 39-065-833-0992
E-mail: aurinfo@aur.edu

U.S. Office

American University of Rome
1025 Connecticut Avenue NW
Suite 601
Washington, D.C. 20036

Phone: 888-791-8327 (toll-free)
Fax: 202-296-9577
E-mail: aurhomeoffice@dc.aur.edu
URL: www.aur.edu

John Cabot University

Rome, Italy

AT A GLANCE

A small American accredited school in the heart of Rome, John Cabot University's education is based on an American liberal arts framework, with especially strong Art History, Business Administration, and International Relations programs. The university's relationships with multinational corporations, embassies, and other organizations offer students many internship employment opportunities.

Undergraduate Enrollment: 406; 50% American, 25% Italian, 25% other nationalities
Male/Female: 61/39
Student/Faculty: 12/1
SAT Scores: Required, but no minimum
Tuition: $11,400 per year
Accreditation: The Commission on Higher Education of the Middle States Association of Colleges and Schools, The Italian Ministry of Public Instruction

---

CAMPUS AND LOCATION

John Cabot University was established in 1972 in a converted convent that consists of three floors and a wing connected by terraces and courtyards. Its grounds are right next door to the gardens of the Academia dei Lincei. The campus is in central Rome in the

Trastevere, a historical and bohemian neighborhood down the river from the Vatican. The neighborhood is crowded and stays up late—one former JCU student compared the young hip area with its cafés, bars, and clubs to New York City's Greenwich Village.

ACADEMICS

Student-teacher rapport is a key element to the JCU education. From freshman year, students are assigned a faculty advisor who guides them through the process of choosing a major and helps them with other aspects of college life. As a result of this system and small class sizes, faculty and students are able to develop tightly knit relationships. But this aspect of academic life can be a double-edged sword: one student remarked that because the campus is so small and there is not much turnover in the faculty, it can be rough if you happen to develop a negative relationship with a professor.

JCU offers Bachelor of Arts degrees in Art History, Business Administration, English Literature, International Affairs, and Political Science. All students take the "General Distribution" program in their freshman and sophomore years, which comprises classes in English composition and literature, and in other areas of the humanities, natural sciences, and social sciences. These introductory courses help to provide students with the foundation they need to be able to choose their major when junior year comes around. The academic year is divided into two semesters of 15 weeks, and students usually take five classes a semester.

Students report that there is a lot of red tape at the university. One student told us that although she had all of her credits, she graduated a semester late because of internal errors. In general, however, students feel that studying at an American school in an international environment offers them an enormous academic advantage.

FACILITIES

The campus houses the computer lab; the newly built Frohling Library, which provides standard reference and academic books as well as thousands of periodicals and on-line research facilities; and the Aula Magna, the largest room in the university, which serves as the theater for the drama club. Some classes are also held in JCU's Sacchetti Building, which is located across the Tiber River in what is known as Rome's *centro storico* (historic center). Students also have full access to the library of the Centro Studi Americani in the Renaissance palazzo Mattei. Since many art history and fine arts classes are conducted at famous sites and monuments, the college considers all of Rome to be its campus.

STUDENT HOUSING AND SERVICES

Housing options at JCU are not too extensive, a fact that has more to do with the lack of affordable space in Rome than with the college itself. University apartments are available in a number of neighborhoods, each offering their own advantages and drawbacks. Because of its proximity to campus and its hopping nightlife, Trastevere is the most popular neighborhood to live in. Unfortunately, housing in this area is very cramped and limited. Other neighborhoods, like Monte Verde, Vatican City, and the area around the Colosseum are quieter and offer larger and more modern facilities but are all about 25 minutes away by bus. The standard housing package is an apartment for up to six students, with a bathroom and kitchen and basic furnishings and two students to a bedroom. Students are not able to choose the neighborhood they live in—they can request to live in a modern or old building, but other than that it's the luck of the draw. JCU also has two residence halls, which are not especially popular because of visitor regulations and curfews. The halls offer amenities like TV, air-conditioning, maid service, and doormen. The university says that it's important to be flexible, but students report that clashes over housing between students and administrators often arise. Room and board costs are generally around $8,000 per year.

As far as support services go, the university offers students free counseling by a licensed psychotherapist. While there are no campus health services, the college can give students references for English-speaking doctors. JCU also offers extensive career services, from job placement to résumé help, and can set students up with a number of volunteer positions around Rome. During the first week of school, the student services office registers all non-European students with the police, which may sound like an insignificant service, but it eliminates having to deal with Italian bureaucracy, an infamously frustrating system.

CAMPUS LIFE

Socially speaking, students have very few complaints about JCU and life in Rome. The campus is small and homey, but surrounded by a big city, so students get the best of both worlds. The student government offers a number of cultural, academic, and sporting activities, as well as trips and special banquets like the annual school-wide Thanksgiving dinner. Rome is a city with endless cultural and historical attractions and great shopping and nightlife. Campo de' Fiori, a big public square surrounded by bars and clubs, is popular with international students, and an after-hours club called Insane is traditionally a big JCU hangout. The international student body makes for an interesting mix as well. Said one student, "There is definitely a social benefit of being able to mingle, study, and live with over 40 different nationalities in a very homey and small campus."

ADMISSIONS AND FINANCIAL INFO

Admission to John Cabot University is selective. Although there are no specific entry requirements, the average GPA of accepted freshmen is 3.0. Apply by July 15 for fall admission and November 21 for spring. Students applying on a semester basis should contact Study Abroad Italy, JCU's study abroad enrollment affiliate (see page 176).

U.S. citizens are entitled to apply for FAFSA, Free Application for Federal Student Aid.

The Sibling Benefits Program provides a tuition reduction for two or more children of the same family attending the university simultaneously. These reductions are given independent of financial need. Some part-time work-study jobs may also be available.

 CONTACTS

John Cabot University in Rome
Via della Lungara 233
00165 Rome
Italy

Phone: 39-06-681-9121
Fax: 39-06-683-2088
E-mail: admissions@johncabot.edu
URL: www.johncabot.edu

U.S. Office

John Cabot University
U.S. Office 101B DeVos
401 W. Fulton Street
Grand Rapids, MI 49504-6431

Phone: 866-277-0112 (toll-free)
Fax: 616-331-7391
E-mail: USoffice@johncabot.edu

STUDY ABROAD ITALY

Study Abroad Italy is the U.S. admissions enrollment office for a number of study abroad centers throughout Italy (as well as for John Cabot University, page 171). The two programs listed below are for semester or yearlong study, and are accredited in the U.S. through Fairfield University in Connecticut. Students are eligible to apply to them directly from high school.

Lorenzo de'Medici /
The Art Institute of Florence

Florence, Italy

AT A GLANCE

The Lorenzo de'Medici School was established in 1973 and has affiliations with a number of American universities. It is the only truly international study abroad program in Italy in that it offers American students the opportunity to study and live with students from around the world.

Enrollment: 700
Male/Female: 1/6
Student/Faculty: 15/1
Tuition: $3,300–$5,500 per semester

CAMPUS AND LOCATION

The Lorenzo de'Medici Center (LDM) is housed in several locations in the San Lorenzo area of Florence, a historic area near such landmarks as the Ponte Vecchio and the Duomo cathedral. Florence is both a historical city and a bustling metropolis with great shopping, restaurants, and nightlife. It offers the most famous Renaissance art museums in the world and is also a major fashion design center. The whole campus area is easily walkable, but Florence also has a fairly reliable public bus system.

ACADEMICS

The academic structure of LDM requires students to choose from a number of set academic programs designed to suit their varying needs (and with varying costs). The Art Block is a set of studio classes taken in a chosen medium. These classes are predetermined by the school, and students may not make any changes whatsoever to the curriculum. The Super Intensive Italian Language program is similar in its rigidity: students take 18 credits in *only* Italian-language classes. The Intensive Italian Language program allows students to take studio art classes as well as some language and non-studio classes, while the Free Elective Block offers the most freedom (and is the most expensive). In this program, students can freely choose from over 200 classes in both academic subjects and fine arts. All programs incorporate at least one Italian-language class into their curriculum, and all programs can be taken for a year or a semester, except the Art Block, which may also be taken as a two- or four-year program. Consult the school's web site at **www.studyabroad-florence.com** for specific program details.

FACILITIES

LDM offers great facilities for artists, such as huge painting studios, photo labs, textile and jewelry design studios, a graphics lab, and regular computer labs. The library is small, but students can register to use any library in Florence, including the English-language library at the British Institute. LDM's main building, which was originally a thirteenth-century convent, contains administrative offices, a café/restaurant, air-conditioned classrooms, studio facilities, reading rooms, three professional kitchens, and a garden.

STUDENT HOUSING AND SERVICES

Students are housed in double or single bedrooms in furnished student apartments, or in homestays with local families. LDM offers a student orientation at the beginning of each term. After that, student advisors assist students with personal, academic, medical, and housing issues.

CAMPUS LIFE

Each semester, LDM organizes group field trips to various Italian cities. These excursions will set you back about $200, including transportation and hotel costs.

Mediterranean Center for the Arts and Sciences

Siracusa, Sicily

AT A GLANCE

This young and impressive semester or yearlong program has the distinction of being the first and only American program in Sicily or southern Italy.

Study Abroad Italy

Enrollment: 30
Male/Female: 1/3
Student/Faculty: 5/1
Tuition: $6,050 per semester

CAMPUS AND LOCATION

The Mediterranean Center is housed in a beautiful fifteenth-century villa by the Mediterranean Sea in Ortigia. The historic center of the town of Syracuse (Siracusa), Ortiga is a small island connected to the mainland by a bridge. The town is relatively small and car traffic is limited, which makes for a welcoming and friendly environment as people pass each other walking through the center of town or hanging out in the piazzas. The Syracuse seaport is lined with cafés where students, travelers, and locals gather. The central marketplace makes shopping for food and other essentials very convenient.

ACADEMICS

The center offers Italian-language classes and courses focused on the modern and ancient Mediterranean world in three areas—Arts (art history and studio arts), Sciences (theoretical and applied), and Humanities. These courses all take full advantage of the resources in the area with many organized trips to historical and cultural sites.

FACILITIES

The fifteenth-century building has been newly renovated to include large classrooms, a computer lab and multimedia room with audio and video facilities, a photography lab, and a lounge situated around a courtyard. Art and Architecture classes are held in the nearby University of Catania's Architecture Department.

STUDENT HOUSING AND SERVICES

The center offers accommodations in shared apartments with single or double rooms. All student housing is inspected by the center and is within walking distance. Apartments come furnished with the essentials, and a cell phone is kept in the apartment for emergencies. Before arriving in Italy, students are given the cell phone number so they can be contacted by anxious parents as soon as they reach their apartments.

While there is no central dining facility, students are given a meal card valid for one meal per day, five days per week, to use in many of the family-run restaurants in town.

The faculty at the small center takes care of all student needs, helping to arrange counseling, health care, and other services. The first three days of the program are designed to thoroughly acclimate students to their new city and surrounding area. The orientation program includes guest speakers, walking tours of the city, and a Sicilian-style feast with faculty members.

CAMPUS LIFE

The Mediterranean Center organizes weekly student activities like theater, sporting, culinary, and musical events, and many events with the local university and the Italian Art Academy, Belle Arti. The center also organizes about four major day and overnight weekend trips a semester. Each semester there are a few extracurricular courses open to the public, providing students with an opportunity to meet locals and European travelers. In the past, some courses offered were Sicilian Cooking and Wine, Sicilian Ceramics and Pottery, and Snorkeling and Diving.

ADMISSIONS AND FINANCIAL INFO FOR ALL
STUDY ABROAD ITALY PROGRAMS

All students must apply through Study Abroad Italy and are generally required to have a 2.5 GPA and a high school diploma. Apply by June 1 for the fall semester and October 1 for spring.

Study Abroad Italy students who receive financial aid from their home institution can usually receive financial aid for programs through an agreement with Fairfield University.

 CONTACTS

Study Abroad Italy
7151 Wilton Avenue, Suite 202
Sebastopol, CA 95472

Phone: 707-824-8965
Toll-free: 800-655-8965
Fax: 707-824-0198
E-mail: mail@studyabroad-italy.com

JAPAN

Center for Japanese Studies, Nanzan University

Nagoya, Japan

AT A GLANCE

Nanzan's Center for Japanese Studies (CJS) is a well-respected semester or yearlong study abroad program that focuses on Japanese language and culture. It is one of the most popular study programs in Japan for American college students.

> **Nanzan University Enrollment:** 6,800
> **CJS Enrollment:** 120; All American
> **CJS Student/Faculty:** 7/1
> **SAT Scores:** Not required
> **CJS Tuition:** $5,660 per year

CAMPUS AND LOCATION

Nanzan University in Nagoya, Japan was founded in 1946 as a college of foreign languages by the Catholic Divine Word Missionaries and the Missionary Sisters of the Holy Spirit. The university is part of the Nanzan Gakuen, an educational complex consisting of the university and its research institutes and study centers, two women's junior colleges, and three high schools. The Center for Japanese Studies (CJS) was founded in 1974.

Nanzan University is situated in the hills over Nagoya, near the cities of Toyota and Seto. Nagoya is a major metropolitan area, with a population of over seven million. Its most famous tourist attraction is the authentically rebuilt seventeenth-century castle. This testament to the city's history is juxtaposed against the skyline of a very modern city with many parks and giant skyscrapers. Nagoya offers many museums and cultural attractions as well as many shopping and dining options. For a phone directory in English, visit **http://english.itp.ne.jp**. Use it to search for businesses, or browse through information on Japanese culture and history and to find city guides and maps.

ACADEMICS

At CJS students take lecture courses on Japanese themes: seminar courses in Social Sciences, Classical Japanese, Translation, Japanese Writing, Business Japanese, Creative Writing, Teaching Japanese as a Foreign Language; and courses in traditional Japanese arts and crafts. CJS students are required to carry a course load of 14–18 credits, including a language class. Second-semester students may be eligible for an independent study program.

FACILITIES

Students at CJS have access to Nanzan's library and computer center, as well as recreational facilities, like the large phys-ed center with an exercise room, judo, squash and basketball courts, a heated pool, an indoor track, outdoor tennis courts, and a baseball field.

STUDENT HOUSING AND SERVICES

CJS students usually participate in homestays with host families in rural areas about 60–90 minutes away from campus by bus (which is a fairly normal commute by Japanese standards). Study abroad students can also choose to live in Nanzan University residence halls with their Japanese peers. Nagoya Koryu Kaikan, one of the more popular residences, accommodates four students (one American CJS student, two international Nanzan students and one native Japanese student) in apartments with single air-conditioned rooms and a shared bathroom and kitchen. The other privately owned dorms have varied facilities with single rooms and no kitchens.

There is a basic health care clinic on campus, but for more specific needs, students are referred to English-speaking doctors in hospitals or clinics near the university. All students are required to register with the Japan National Health Insurance Program, because Japanese medical facilities will not usually accept foreign insurance. The center for international education provides personal and academic advice, and the CJS dean of student affairs is available for counseling and guidance. The Nanzan Logos Center and the Nanzan Church provide services and spiritual support.

CAMPUS LIFE

CJS sponsors many extracurricular activities like field trips to museums and visits to zen monasteries and kabuki theaters. CJS students are encouraged to participate in clubs and extracurricular activities with the rest of the Nanzan student body. The Nanzan Passion Play, the heart of Nanzan's spiritual tradition, is performed annually by over 200 students under the direction of the Passion Play Club members.

ADMISSIONS AND FINANCIAL INFO

The Center for Japanese Studies accepts any student with a 3.0 GPA, but priority is given to college students and students with some Japanese training. Students coming directly from a U.S. high school must show exceptional desire and ability or already be admitted to a university in the States. Apply by March 31 for the fall semester and by August 31 for the spring semester. Contact CJS for information on financial aid.

CONTACTS

Center for Japanese Studies
Nanzan University
18 Yamazato-cho Showa-ku
Nagoya 466-8673
Japan

Phone: 81-052-832-3111
Fax: 81-052-832-6983
E-mail: n-somu@nanzan-u.ac.jp
URL: www.ic.nanzan-u.ac.jp/English

KENYA

United States International University, Nairobi Campus

Nairobi, Kenya

AT A GLANCE

USIU Nairobi Campus is an international branch of Alliant International University, a business school in San Diego. Students come to the relatively large Nairobi campus for the International Business Administration and Information Systems programs, but stay for the tight-knit community atmosphere and beautiful campus. (See also Alliant International University, Mexico City Campus, page 200.)

Total Enrollment: 2,506; 10% international
Undergraduate Enrollment: 2,163
Male/Female: 46/54
SAT Scores: Required, but no minimum
Tuition: $4,576 per year
Room and Board: $2,964
Accreditation: Western Association of Schools and Colleges, Commission for Higher Education in Kenya

CAMPUS AND LOCATION

USIU's Nairobi Campus was founded in 1962 as the first secular university in East Africa. In 1991, the university relocated to its current spot in Kasarani. The new 20-acre campus is green and lush with its modern single-story buildings nestled under Jacaranda trees and bougainvillea. The campus is located about 40 minutes from the Jomo Kenyatta International Airport and 20 minutes from downtown Nairobi.

Nairobi (population 2.1 million) is the capital of Kenya and the country's main commercial and cultural center. English and Swahili are its official languages, but many indigenous languages are also spoken in the area. The big city can sometimes be dangerous, especially for foreigners who can make easy targets if they're not careful. Students reported that it is especially important to be street smart, and to watch out for locals who might seem overly eager to help out a tourist. On the other hand, one student said that the best way to exchange money is to enlist a trustworthy local to do it for you on the black market—a very common practice, and one that yields a much better exchange rate.

Outside of the city, Kenya is known for its stunning scenic views and wildlife, found in the country's many game and marine parks.

ACADEMICS

The School of Arts and Sciences and the School of Business Administration offer degrees in the following areas: Business Administration, International Business Administration, Information Systems and Technology, Journalism, International Relations, Psychology, Tourism Management, and Hotel and Restaurant Management. Classes are reported to be small, with a lot of personalized attention from professors. Said one alum, "The learning was non-patronizing; we were encouraged to question, speak our minds, and critique. I felt armed with the confidence to exploit my full potential." Many degree programs also require internships, which are set up through the school with local business firms.

FACILITIES

Academic facilities at USIU are some of the best in the area. The computer labs are state-of-the-art, and the Lillian Beam Library offers a large number of volumes, on-line periodicals, and an inter-library loan with other libraries in the area. To reciprocate, USIU has opened its facilities to students from other universities in Nairobi, and they come mainly to use the modern gym with a weight and aerobics room, the basketball courts, and the rugby fields. The campus restaurant and café are reported to be not so appetizing, but we hear that the new president is working on getting it up to par.

STUDENT HOUSING AND SERVICES

USIU has two traditional dorms that accommodate about 300 people, with priority given to international students. The hostels, as they are called, house students in double rooms with shared bathrooms, and each has a TV/Ping-Pong room and a live-in resident assistant. Most students prefer to live off campus, because it's cheaper and better for socializing, but they report that dealing with setting up utilities, especially a phone line, can be "a huge headache."

Support services are somewhat limited. For a fee of $80 a year, students have access to the campus health center, and the career counseling center offers workshops and job placement assistance.

CAMPUS LIFE

When asked about extracurricular activities on campus, one enthusiastic administrator said, "Students never run out of things to do where activities are concerned. It is a beehive!" Students can get involved in the community through a variety of service activities. (One hundred hours of community service are required for graduation.) Some of the most popular programs work with children's homes and hospitals, such as the Abandoned Baby Center, Homeless Children International, and Bread for Children. Many student clubs organize activities like workshops, career days, and campus and community cleanups. There are also theme days sponsored by international embassies in Kenya (in the past, Saudi Arabia Day and Poland Day) and other university-wide activities like the annual Mini-Olympics, the Mr. and Miss USIU contest, safari trips (reported to be very worthwhile), the Vice Chancellor's BBQ, and the quarterly Freshers' Bash. The Nairobi campus also has varsity and intramural rugby, basketball, hockey, soccer, and swimming teams.

Off campus students live it up, too. One student wrote, "I had such a great time that I never wanted to go to class!" The nightlife in Nairobi is great, and students enjoy hanging out at the many bars, restaurants, and clubs, citing Florida 2000 as an especially popular local club and Trattoria as a great Italian restaurant.

ADMISSIONS AND FINANCIAL INFO

Applicants must have a 2.5 GPA and submit two letters of recommendation and a two-page essay along with the application form. Students apply directly through AIU San Diego, which has an ongoing enrollment policy.

Some financial aid may be available to American students through the university's San Diego campus. A 15% tuition discount is granted to two students enrolled from the same family, and a 25% discount is offered to three or more students from the same family. Students who introduce other students to the university receive a 10% tuition discount when the other student enrolls.

CONTACTS

United States International University, Nairobi
P.O. Box 14634
Thika Road, Kasarani
Nairobi
Kenya

Phone: 25-42-3606-000
Fax: 25-42-3606-100
E-mail: admit@usiu.ac.ke
URL: www.usiu.ac.ke

U.S. Office

**Alliant University Fulfillment Office/
  Systemwide Admissions**
10455 Pomerado Road
San Diego, CA 92131

Phone: 866-U-ALLIANT
E-mail: admissions@alliant.edu
URL: www.alliant.edu

LEBANON

American University of Beirut

Beirut, Lebanon

AT A GLANCE

The American University of Beirut is thought by many of its students to be one of the best American universities abroad. Since before the turn of the century, it has been dedicated to making a top-notch American-accredited education accessible to its predominantly Middle Eastern students.

Total Enrollment: 6,600; 18% international
Undergraduate Enrollment: 4,964
Male/Female: 55/45
Student/Faculty: 12/1
SAT Scores: 1150 average
Tuition: $8,000–$11,000 per year
Accreditation: The Commission on Higher Education of the Middle States Association of Colleges and Schools

---

CAMPUS AND LOCATION

The American University of Beirut was started by a charter from the State of New York in 1866, with one class of 16 students. Since then

LEBANON

it has developed into a large and respected research-oriented university incorporating a School of Medicine, Faculty of Arts and Sciences, Faculty of Engineering and Health Sciences, Faculty of Agricultural and Food Sciences, Faculty of Health Sciences, and the American University Hospital and School of Nursing. In 2001, AUB was granted American accreditation by the Commission on Higher Education of the Middle States Association of Colleges and Schools.

AUB's campus is situated on over 70 acres on the Ras Beirut Peninsula along the Mediterranean Sea. The beautiful green and flowering campus (with its own private beach and bird sanctuary) is protected by six entrance gates, each with a posted security guard. The administration emphasizes the many safety precautions that are taken on campus because of the high-profile nature of many of AUB's students (children of diplomats, politicians, and important businessmen). Even during recent years of civil unrest in Beirut, admissions representatives say that the AUB campus was the safest place in the city.

Beirut is characterized by the presence of military guards, and it is advised for foreigners to carry identification papers (your passport or visa) at all times. Surprisingly enough though, the cosmopolitan city is thought by many inhabitants and visitors to be far safer than a lot of other major cities around the world, at least in terms of street crime. One of the only complaints that students had about the city was the pollution level: nearly every student we talked to said that the smog was the worst thing about living in Beirut. Beirut is very cosmopolitan, and the AUB campus, located in Ras Beirut, is near many cultural centers (such as the Goethe Institute and the British Institute), English-language bookstores, and all kinds of restaurants (including KFC, Pizza Hut, and Ben and Jerry's, for those of you who get homesick). The city possesses a wealth of history and scenic beauty and is home to many monuments and temples dating back to before the Common Era.

ACADEMICS

The university offers bachelor's degrees in the faculties of Arts and Sciences, Medicine (and the School of Nursing), Health Sciences,

Agricultural and Food Sciences, and Engineering and Architecture. Core curricula and requirements vary depending on the faculty.

Some students say that at AUB you get the best of both worlds— an American curriculum that emphasizes creative thinking, taught by Lebanese professors who are thought to be tougher than their American counterparts. On the down side, one student mentioned that the grading system is so hard that it's sometimes difficult to get into European or American graduate programs.

FACILITIES

AUB is very well set up. It has two main libraries: the Saab Memorial Medical Library and the Jafet Memorial Library, which has three branches. The university has its own publications office as well as an archeological museum (one of the oldest museums in the Middle East), a large collection provided by the biology department in Beirut's Natural History Museum, a large and impressive herbarium, and the only geological collection in Lebanon.

STUDENT HOUSING AND SERVICES

AUB prides itself on being able to offer traditional American "dorm life" to its primarily Middle Eastern students (although only about 20% of all students live on campus). The administration describes the residence halls as "stable and nostalgic beautiful stone buildings," offering students a sense of history and tradition. Some students, however, feel that the dorms are in need of a makeover, and one especially harsh student said that in Jewett, one of the women's dorms, there were "more insects than residents." On the other hand, another student told us that some dorms have recently been renovated and are very comfortable. In any case, dorm life at AUB is not quite like it is at American universities. Although not as strict as some universities in the Middle East (like the American University in Cairo, page 111), AUB keeps a close watch over its students in residence. Students must be in the dorms between 12 A.M. (1 A.M. on weekends) and 7 A.M., although parents can sign a form to have the curfew waived. There are no coed dorms, men and women are not allowed in each other's rooms, and there is no alcohol or smoking permitted. Each of the six halls (four women's, two men's) has a ground floor with a reception area, computers with internet access, a TV lounge, international pay phones, vending machines, and laundry facilities. Students can opt for private rooms, semi-private rooms, or doubles.

AUB students receive health care through the American University hospital. It is located on campus and is one of the best facilities of its kind in the region. The AUB counseling center provides students with professional psychological counseling.

CAMPUS LIFE

Be it on or off campus, there is lots going on at AUB. There are about 30 registered student clubs at AUB, mostly cultural and academic, but also some recreational, like yoga, folk music, and dancing. But don't expect to find anything like a gay or lesbian club on this conservative campus. One student even complained to us about the amount of PDA (public displays of affection, for those of you who may have forgotten the term). Each residence hall plans a number of social activities throughout the year to ensure that students feel a sense of community. There are open houses, ski trips, a New Year's Party, theme nights and outdoor activities in the spring, and a big graduation party. There is also a weekly student newspaper and an annual yearbook. Off campus, students generally head to Monot Street for clubs and bars, Bliss street for cafés and sandwich shops, and Beirut's bustling downtown area for shopping.

ADMISSIONS AND FINANCIAL INFO

American students should apply through the New York office. Each year the university awards ten full-tuition merit scholarships, but generally financial aid is need-based. Work-study programs are available, and about 10% of the student body participate in them. Contact the New York office for details.

CONTACTS

American University of Beirut
Michael Lyons, Director of International Students
Ada Dodge Hall
P.O. Box 11-0236
Riad El Solh
Beirut 1107 2020
Lebanon

Phone: 961-1-340460
Fax: 961-1-351706
E-mail: mlyons@aub.edu.lb
URL: www.aub.edu.lb

U.S. Office

American University of Beirut
Julie Millstein, Assistant to the President
3 Dag Hammarskjold Plaza, 8th floor
New York, NY 10017-2303

Phone: 212-583-7600
Fax: 212-583-7650
E-mail: mills@aub.edu

MALTA

University of Malta

Msida, Malta

AT A GLANCE

Although relatively small, the University of Malta offers students a wide array of services, facilities, programs, and extracurricular organizations, all in a beautiful Mediterranean island setting. Academics are heavily research-oriented and emphasize independent learning. The campus is the hub of international relations and research for the Maltese islands.

Undergraduate Enrollment: 8,000; 90 American, 710 other nationalities
Male/Female: 45/55
Tuition: $4,500–$6,200 per year

CAMPUS AND LOCATION

The University of Malta's campus is located on the island of Malta, which is situated in the Mediterranean Sea between Sicily and North Africa. The Maltese civilization dates back to about 5000 B.C., and Malta is home to many ancient ruins and temple sites. With a population of about 350,000, Malta is the biggest of the three Maltese Islands (the other two are Gozo and Comino). Its official languages are Maltese and English, although most people are also fluent in Italian. Its history, beauty, and perfect Mediterranean climate make the country a popular European vacation spot, and the island is full of restaurants, cafés, bars, and hotels. A reliable public transportation system provides a cheap and effective way to get around the island. For more on Malta, go to **www.visitmalta.com**.

ACADEMICS

The University of Malta offers undergraduate degrees across ten faculties: Architecture and Civil Engineering; Arts; Dental Surgery; Economics, Management and Accountancy; Education; Engineering; Law; Medicine and Surgery; Science; and Theology. These faculties are divided into more than 50 different departments. The University of Malta also offers some undergraduate courses through a number of specialized institutes and centers, including the European Documentation and Research Center, the Institute of Anglo-Italian Studies, the International Institute for Baroque Studies, the Institute for Energy Technology, the Institute for Masonry and Construction Research, and the Mediterranean Academy of Diplomatic Studies. Most undergraduate courses are made up of lectures, tutorials, labs and fieldwork, and individual study units. These individual study units are assigned one or more credits a year, with each credit equal to 50 hours of study, of which only 14 hours are supervised by a professor. Assignments and tests are given at the end of each study unit. Under this system, students who are not self-motivated may find themselves flailing by the end of the year, but students who can work on their own find that they become serious scholars in their field.

The Foundation for International Studies is the international relations branch of the University of Malta. It functions as an autonomous institution to promote international research, training, and study for the University of Malta and the Maltese population. The foundation includes the Islands and Small States Institute, the International Environment Institute, the Future Generations Program, and the Euro-Mediterranean Center on Insular Coastal Dynamics.

FACILITIES

The university library houses half a million books and is fully computerized. (Check out its card catalog at **www.lib.um.edu.mt**.)

There are also a number of sports facilities on campus—a newly built heated Olympic-size pool and separate diving pool, a football (i.e., soccer) field, three outdoor tennis courts, and a sports pavilion that houses billiard tables, a darts room, Ping-Pong tables, and a small fitness center.

STUDENT HOUSING AND SERVICES

Student housing is extremely cushy. University dorms are located in the village of Lija, about seven miles away from central campus. (A 24-hour shuttle bus service is provided.) The Lija residences have a laundromat, a mini market, a coffee bar, a cafeteria, a swimming pool, a tennis court, a jogging track, a TV lounge, a computer room, and a photocopy service. Students live in three-bedroom apartments with a shared kitchen, bathroom, and common space. A maid comes once a week to clean and to change the linens and towels. Room and board will set you back only $2,340 per year for a single and $1,560 per year for a double.

The university provides extensive support services to its students. Academic counseling and private psychological counseling is available, and workshops and therapy groups are organized to address students' personal issues. The university is also committed to making its facilities accessible to disabled students. A number of motorized wheelchairs and implements for the visually and hearing impaired are available, and part-time facilitators are assigned to help disabled students. The International Office organizes orientation activities, like day trips around the Maltese Islands and a welcome party to help new students meet the rest of the student body. The international office also helps international students register for classes.

CAMPUS LIFE

Aside from the beach, historical sites, and tourist activities that Malta is famous for, students can get involved in a number of organized clubs and associations on campus, such as the university music association, the society for African Studies, Amnesty International, MUSC (an athletics club that offers all kinds of sports imaginable), an anthropology society that organizes films, lectures, seminars, and ethnic meals, and a film club that shows movies every Saturday night. For students who are looking to stretch their legs, Malta is the perfect starting-off point for traveling to southern Europe and northern Africa.

ADMISSIONS AND FINANCIAL INFO

Certain courses have special entry requirements, but for general undergraduate admission, U.S. students are required to have a high school diploma as well as three AP test scores. Apply by June 30 for the fall semester.

The University of Malta does not offer any scholarships or financial aid to overseas students, and international students are not eligible for any part-time work (even on campus) while they are studying in Malta.

 CONTACTS

Foundation for International Studies
University of Malta
St. Paul Street, Valletta VLT 07
Malta

Phone: 35-6-2123-4121 ext. 217
Fax: 35-6-2123-0538
E-mail: intoff@um.edu.mt
URL: www.um.edu.mt

MEXICO

Alliant International University, Mexico City Campus

Mexico City, Mexico

AT A GLANCE

Alliant International University in San Diego is a little-known business school with campuses around the world. The Mexico City campus focuses on international relations, international business, and languages. Students love the small campus for its sense of community and the welcoming atmosphere of Mexico City. (See also the Nairobi campus, page 186.)

Undergraduate Enrollment: 85
Average Class Size: 12–15
SAT Scores: Required for financial aid applicants only
Tuition: $2,304–$2,800 per semester
Accreditation: Western Association of Schools and Colleges

CAMPUS AND LOCATION

Alliant International University's Mexico City campus was founded in 1970 as an international branch of AIU in San Diego. The campus is located in one building in Colonia Roma, a neighborhood known as Mexico City's main cultural area. The campus is surrounded by turn-of-the-century buildings, housing cafés, museums, and theaters. Students unanimously love the city, which is a culturally and socially diverse metropolis. The beautiful weather, beaches, cheap prices, delicious food, and laid-back and friendly atmosphere are just a few aspects of the city that students fall in love with. Although Mexico City can be a bit crowded and dangerous, one student said that this forced her to learn the language more quickly so as not to be an easy target. Cheap and reliable public buses and subways make it easy to travel around.

ACADEMICS

AIU offers B.A.s in International Business Administration, International Relations, Latin American Studies, and Psychology and minors in several more subjects. Students are generally very pleased with the level of academics, although some students feel that if the campus offered more majors it would attract a more diverse student body. Classes are small and require a lot of active participation. All students are required to take 86 units of General Education requirements, which include natural and social sciences and humanities. Taken in the first year or two, these courses are designed to provide students with a strong academic foundation and help them meet the requirements of American universities in case they want to transfer back to the States.

All students must also participate in an internship or community service program in which they spend 120 hours working for one of AIU's affiliate companies (business or nonprofit, depending on the student's major) while under the supervision of an AIU faculty member. AIU also offers an interesting program called Academic Tours where students travel with professors to specific areas of Mexico for intensive classes in a related area.

FACILITIES

Facilities at AIU are somewhat limited, which students say is the campus's main drawback. Student can use the Alliant library and computer lab, as well as other libraries in the Mexico City area including the large Benjamin Franklin Library of the U.S. embassy. The computer lab is located in the Alliant library and is designated primarily for class usage. A neighboring internet café makes up for the lack of computers on campus.

STUDENT HOUSING AND SERVICES

There are no dorms on campus, which students say are badly needed, but the university does offer students a lot of assistance in setting up apartment shares with other students or homestays with Mexican families. For temporary housing, AIU places students in a three-star hotel down the street that offers special rates.

Student services are not extensive, but because the campus is so small and friendly, students say that you can pretty much ask any faculty member for whatever kind of assistance you may need.

CAMPUS LIFE

To put it simply, students at AIU Mexico are happy. When asked to describe the student body, one student told us, "When you come to our campus you feel like you're in a different world—different dress and languages, and everyone smiles with joy." The small student body is very diverse, allowing students the opportunity to become friends with people from all over the world. There are also plenty of things to do in Mexico City. The school is near the Zona Condesa, an area known for its trendy bars and atmospheric dining. The university also encourages students to soak up Mexican culture by organizing excursions and extracurricular language programs as well as a special cultural training program.

ADMISSIONS AND FINANCIAL INFO

See United States International University, Nairobi page 189.

CONTACTS

Alliant International University Mexico City Campus
Alvaro Obregón #110
Colonia Roma, CP 06700
Mexico DF
Mexico

Phone: 52-55-5264-2187
Fax: 52-55-5264-2188
E-mail: admissions@usiumexico.edu
URL: www.usiumexico.edu

U.S. Office

Alliant University Fulfillment Office/
  Systemwide Admissions
10455 Pomerado Road
San Diego, CA 92131

Phone: 866-U-ALLIANT
E-mail: admissions@alliant.edu
URL: www.alliant.edu

MONACO

International University of Monaco

Monaco

AT A GLANCE

Is there a more appropriate way to study the art of making money (a.k.a. business management) than on the French Riviera, rubbing elbows with the fabulously rich? IUM prides itself on offering an American-accredited education in an intimate and beautiful setting.

Total Enrollment: 300
Undergraduate Enrollment: 170
Male/Female: 50/50
Average Class Size: 20
SAT Scores: Not required
Tuition: $6,124 per semester
Accreditation: The Accrediting Council for Independent Colleges and Schools (ACICS), The Government of the Principality of Monaco

---

CAMPUS AND LOCATION

The university was founded in 1986 as the University of Southern Europe, but was renamed the International University of Monaco in 2001 when it changed ownership. The small campus is located in Monaco, an independent sovereign state in the south of France between the southern Alps and the Mediterranean. (In 1957, the beloved Hollywood star Grace Kelly brought the state into the public eye when she married Monaco's Prince Rainier and became a princess.) The thirteenth-century seaside town is known for its glittering casinos and gorgeous beaches. The playground of the European jet set, there is no lack of things to do, although many students feel a bit out of place among the elite inhabitants. One student said, "the weather and beaches are amazing, and the people-watching is great, but going out amongst the rich and beautiful can be totally intimidating sometimes." For a cool comprehensive English guide to life on the Côte d'Azur (as the French Riviera is known), visit **www.angloinfo.com.**

ACADEMICS

IUM's business education combines the rigid structure of a European university with a pragmatic American approach (i.e., lots of case studies). The goal is to make students feel comfortable in the wide world of international business.

The university offers two degrees: a Bachelor of Arts in Business and E-Commerce (BeCom) and a Bachelor of Science in Business Administration (BSBA). The BSBA program is intended to familiarize students with all areas of business studies. It requires a number of interdisciplinary courses in management, marketing, finance, accounting, economics, strategy, and quantitative analysis. The BeCom program focuses on information technology, marketing, international trade, and languages to prepare students to meet the challenges of globalization. First-year BeCom students must take prerequisite English Skills (ENGL 1000) and Preparatory Mathematics (MATH 1000) courses.

Both degree programs are made up of 39 courses, require two internships and a thesis, and may be completed in less than four years with summer sessions. All undergraduate students are also required to take courses in two foreign languages: French, German,

Spanish, or Italian. The vast majority of students report that they actually become bilingual by the time they graduate.

Classes are small, allowing students to build strong relationships with their professors. In fact, many adjunct faculty members are business executives who both instruct and mentor students. Teaching combines lectures, case studies, practical research, and many field trips for on-site research.

FACILITIES

When IUM changed hands a few years ago, its facilities were majorly revamped. Classrooms and the main library were refurbished with snazzy furniture, new computers, and other state-of-the-art technology. The university also expanded and improved the library's electronic database.

STUDENT HOUSING AND SERVICES

IUM houses students in two residences in Beaulieu-sur-Mer (translation: beautiful place on the sea), a small town between Nice and Monaco that is about a 15-minute train ride from campus. These "dorms" are very cushy: they consist of fully furnished studios with kitchens in modern apartment complexes, complete with a TV room and laundry facilities. The nearby shopping area, tennis courts, beach, and train station keep students from feeling isolated.

Student services helps set students up in residences and open bank accounts in Monaco. They assist with visa applications, official residence papers, and health insurance and can also refer students to doctors in the area. Career, academic, and personal counseling is available as well.

CAMPUS LIFE

IUM's Student Association sponsors many clubs and activities, and is dedicated to giving back to the community by raising money for local charities and organizing volunteer events.

ADMISSIONS AND FINANCIAL INFO

Applying requires a $130 fee and an interview once all other application materials (essay, transcripts, test scores, etc.) are received. Phone interviews can be arranged for international applicants. Apply by June 15 for fall admission, October 15 for spring.

CONTACTS

Grisel Damgaard, Nadine Fevre, and Jean-Marc Rouhier
International University of Monaco
2, avenue du Prince Héréditaire Albert
MC 98000
Principality of Monaco

Phone: 37-79-7986-986
Fax: 37-79-2052-830
E-mail: info@monaco.edu
URL: www.monaco.edu

NETHERLANDS

Webster University Netherlands

Leiden, Netherlands

AT A GLANCE

Webster University, "where professors love to teach," is based in St. Louis, and like Schiller International University (see page 125), it is an international business-oriented American university with many overseas campuses. Although we only feature its two most comprehensive campuses (see also Webster Thailand on page 237), Webster has over 100 study centers around the world, mostly on army bases.

Total Enrollment: 250
Undergraduate Enrollment: 230; 20% American
Male/Female: 50/50
Average Class Size: 20
SAT Scores: Not required
Tuition: $8,500 per year
Accreditation: North Central Association of Colleges and Schools

CAMPUS AND LOCATION

Webster's Netherlands campus, founded in 1983, is housed in a small eighteenth-century two-story building on the main canal in the heart of Leiden. The building is very homey, with message boards and student notices taped to walls, reflecting the university's tight-knit community spirit. Leiden, a small and picturesque college town, has been dubbed "Little Amsterdam" for its wide canals, great shopping, and many bars and cafés (there are even a few "coffee shops"). Webster shares turf with the University of Leiden, the oldest established Dutch university, which is largely responsible for the bustling youthful vibe in this small town. It also generously allows the teeny Webster University to share all of its facilities.

ACADEMICS

Across all its campuses, Webster prides itself on hiring professors who are almost all professionals in their field. The university feels that this helps give students an idea of the practical applications of their majors. It also ensures that the professors are truly dedicated—they have willingly taken time out of their busy work schedules to teach. Students feel that their education at Webster is an active one. Classes are small and discussion-oriented, and there are many guest speakers, case studies, and group oral presentations. Business studies are interdisciplinary and touch on a wide range of subjects like psychology, law, and politics.

The Netherlands campus offers undergraduate degrees in art history, business administration, business and management, media communications, and psychology. (Art history and media communications students are required to complete their degree at the St. Louis campus.) The school year is divided into three eight-week terms, and most classes are offered day or night. Students are required to take a core curriculum made up of nine classes. Full-time students generally have about 12 hours of class time a week, and 25 hours of work outside the classroom.

Webster promotes dual majors and study abroad in order to make students seem as interesting and well-rounded as possible to future employers. The university offers a one-year study abroad cultural immersion program where students take a variety of classes in the arts and humanities.

FACILITIES

To call the Webster Netherlands campus small would be something of an understatement. All of its classrooms and offices as well as the library and computer lab are located in one beautifully restored eighteenth-century two-story building on Leiden's main canal. The campus bookstore and cafeteria are located nearby, and Webster students also have access to all of the University of Leiden's facilities.

STUDENT HOUSING AND SERVICES

Students share an international residence hall with Leiden University. Webster University also recently bought and converted a few houses in town that act as dorms, but they are smaller and do not offer interaction with Dutch students. Shared facilities in all dorms include a shower for every four rooms, a bathroom for every two rooms, a kitchen for every five rooms, and laundry facilities.

Most students' support needs are met through the Office of Student Affairs in the main building. There is no health center, but all Webster University students must have health insurance, and if they do not have it already, they will be automatically billed for the Webster University Student Health Plan.

CAMPUS LIFE

There are a number of student clubs at Webster, including a dance club, the Association for African American Collegians, the Art Council, and the Fellowship of Christian Athletes. Because Webster University Netherlands is so small, students have a very easy time setting up clubs and can get help from the student activities staff. Off campus Leiden is a total university town, the majority of its inhabitants are students, and there are tons of pubs, cafés, and students hanging out everywhere.

ADMISSIONS AND FINANCIAL INFO

Students apply through the main campus in St. Louis and must have a minimum 2.5 GPA. Webster University offers some academic scholarships, as well as grants, loans, and work-study programs. Contact the St. Louis office for details.

 CONTACTS

Webster University—The Netherlands
Boommarkt 1
2311 EA Leiden
Netherlands

Phone: 31-71-514-4341
E-mail: info@webster.nl
URL: www.webster.nl

Webster University
Office of Undergraduate Admissions
470 East Lockwood Avenue
St. Louis, MO 63119-3194

Phone: 314-968-6991
Toll-free: 1-800-75-ENROLL
Fax: 314-968-7115
URL: www.webster.edu

SINGAPORE

National University of Singapore

Singapore

AT A GLANCE

National University of Singapore is a very large and prestigious science-oriented university that offers internationally recognized undergraduate degrees as well as exchanges and alliances with American universities like MIT, Harvard, UPenn, Stanford, and Johns Hopkins. The range of facilities and services at NUS are as impressive as its academics are.

Total Enrollment: 32,145
Undergraduate Enrollment: 23,137
SAT Scores: 550 Verbal, 650 Math required
Tuition: $3,586 per year

CAMPUS AND LOCATION

Founded in 1905, the National University of Singapore is one of Singapore's first universities. NUS's original (if somewhat dry) name, The Straits Settlements and Federated Malay States Government Medical School, was changed to its current moniker in 1980 after a merger with the Nanyang University. Since then, NUS has

National University of Singapore

become a prestigious international center for research and achievement in the applied sciences. NUS's vast main campus at Kent Ridge spans about 250 landscaped acres in a convenient area of Singapore about 20 minutes away from the airport. Singapore, an island with 63 surrounding islets, is one of the busiest ports in the world. The city-state was founded in 1819 as a British colony, joined Malaysia in 1963, and then declared its independence two years later in 1965. Four official languages are spoken in Singapore—English, Malay, Mandarin, and Tamil—but most locals speak a mélange of foreign slang and English. For some very basic tourist information on the city go to **www.visitsingapore.com**.

ACADEMICS

NUS's ten undergraduate faculties—Arts and Social Sciences, Business, Computing, Dentistry, Design and Environment, Engineering, Law, Medicine, Science, and the Singapore Conservatory of Music—offer hundreds of undergraduate degree programs. The university's academic program is based on modules, which the university says gives students the intensity of the British educational system combined with the flexibility of an American system. Each semester students must fulfill elective modules as well as specific modules for their faculty.

The university also has a few study centers in the U.S. At the NUS campus in central Philadelphia, students can spend one year as interns at computer companies while taking classes at the University of Pennsylvania's School of Engineering and Applied Science (SEAS) and the Wharton School of Business. NUS has a similar program in Silicon Valley that combines an internship with two entrepreneurship courses at the Stanford University School of Engineering. All full-time NUS undergraduates who have completed two years of study are eligible to apply for these programs.

FACILITIES

NUS lives up to its reputation as an intense research-oriented university by offering very comprehensive academic facilities. The Kent Ridge campus library system is made up of six libraries: the Central

Library, the Chinese Library, the C J Koh Law Library, the Hon Sui Sen Memorial Library, the Medical Library, and the Science Library. There are 12 university-level and 12 NUS-affiliated national-level research centers, as well as computer labs that include a supercomputing and visualization center. The arts are represented by the Center for the Arts, the NUS museum, and the University Cultural Center, a large performing arts venue. Sports facilities are extensive and feature playing fields, tennis courts, indoor gyms, air-conditioned weight and aerobics rooms, and an outdoor swimming center with its own cafeteria. Many dining facilities (with interesting names like the Grinning Gecko, Techno Edge, and Cool Station) are located around campus.

STUDENT HOUSING AND SERVICES

NUS has six halls of residence that provide housing for about 5,000 students. Facilities vary across the halls, but the largest, the PGP residence, gives students a choice of three different types of single rooms: air-conditioned with a private bathroom, non-air-conditioned with a sink, and standard (i.e., without air conditioner or sink). All international students are given housing priority for their first two years at the university. For those who want to stay off campus, residential services helps students find alternative housing with roommates and in homestay arrangements.

Comprehensive student services include employment and career counseling, personal guidance and counseling, international student services, and a health service clinic that includes a pharmacy and surgery facilities.

CAMPUS LIFE

The National University of Singapore Students' Union (NUSSU) is the university's official student group. The union, governed by the union council, looks out for the welfare of its students and organizes many (mainly academic) extracurricular clubs. For the student union web site, visit **www.nussu.nus.edu.sg**.

Students looking to express their artistic side at this science-oriented university can take advantage of an extensive extracurricular arts program offered at the Center for the Arts. Spectators can check out the University Cultural Center, which hosts performances by professional and student music, dance, and drama companies.

Off campus, students enjoy partying at the many clubs in town. Zouk is reported to be especially popular with NUS's international students, and one American student mentioned that the weekly party organized by marines at the American embassy is fun. Students also enjoy taking time away from their studies to travel throughout southeast Asia.

ADMISSIONS AND FINANCIAL INFO

Students with American high school qualifications must submit their SAT scores as well as scores from three SAT II tests—English, math, and a third subject that corresponds with the course they're applying for at NUS. (Scores can be faxed directly to the university or sent through ETS.) Apply by March 1 for the fall semester.

International freshmen may apply for the merit-based NUS undergraduate scholarship worth $2,479 per year.

 CONTACTS

Office of Admissions
National University of Singapore
University Hall Level 2
10 Kent Ridge Crescent
Singapore 119260

Phone: 65-6874-8968/4356
Fax: 65-6778-7570
E-mail: enquire@nus.edu.sg
URL: www.nus.edu.sg

SOUTH AFRICA

University of Cape Town
Rondebosch, South Africa

AT A GLANCE

The University of Cape Town (UCT) was founded in 1829 as an all-boys secondary school, and over the years has developed into a well-respected university with an emphasis on postgraduate work. The large school is South Africa's oldest and most prestigious university, and has continuously flourished in the face of the country's many decades of political turmoil, all the while sustaining its opposition to apartheid.

Total Enrollment: 19,000
Undergraduate Enrollment: 13,200
Male/Female: 52/48
Tuition: $5,300–$6,000 per year
Accreditation: South African Ministry of Education

CAMPUS AND LOCATION

In the history of the university, UCT's campus is relatively new, having moved in 1928 to its current location on the slopes of Devil's Peak, one of Africa's southernmost points. The surrounding suburban town of Rondebosch offers a vibrant social and outdoor lifestyle—mountain walks, theaters, restaurants, and student-minded activities abound. For more info on Rondebosch, known as the "student suburb," visit **www.rondebosch.co.za**.

The campus is only a few miles from Cape Town, a bustling metropolis with a strong cultural scene, trendy shopping areas, and great nightlife. It is also a city that remembers its history of imperialism, colonialism, and intense political struggle. The neat Dutch houses and well-manicured vineyards that give Cape Town a European flavor contrast sharply with neighboring townships like Langa, Crossroads, and Khayelitsha, which have been devastated by the effects of apartheid. South Africa has 11 official languages, but you can get by on English alone. The Cape Town region is also entirely free from malaria (as the tourist bureau is quick to point out). For more information on the city, visit **www.cape-town-south-africa-holidays.com**.

ACADEMICS

The University of Cape Town has six main academic faculties: Commerce, Engineering, Health Sciences, Humanities, Law, and Science. As with many large universities, classes are often taught as huge impersonal lectures. One student told us that the few grad seminars he was able to take were much more involved, with better professors and more student participation. UCT's general academic framework is made up of lectures, seminars, and tutorials, and students are expected to be self-motivated and to be able to work independently.

FACILITIES

The UCT library system is made up of the main Chancellor Oppenheimer Library and its smaller branch libraries, as well as the newly built Knowledge Commons, a state-of-the-art research center with a computer lab. There are also many general computer labs around campus. The Center for African Studies houses the UCT art gallery, and the university's sports center houses the sports administration and clubs as well as a sports injury clinic.

STUDENT HOUSING AND SERVICES

There are only 4,500 campus residence spots for UCT's 19,000 students, so needless to say, most students live off campus. Housing priority is given to international students, many of whom enjoy the ready-made communities in the dorms. A variety of housing options is available through UCT's three-tier housing system, which is designed to give students more independence gradually as they get older. The first tier is for students under 21 and has no kitchen facilities but offers three meals a day in the campus dining hall. The second tier has kitchen facilities, as does the third tier, for seniors and grad students, which is not managed by a warden as the other residences are.

UCT encourages students to take advantage of university support resources from their first year on. UCT's center for higher education development includes the academic development program, the writing center, the career development program, and the multimedia education group, all of which work across the university's faculties to improve the quality of teaching and learning. The writing center also coordinates student learning centers, located across campus, which house computers with internet access, study rooms, and other academic resources.

Student health services provides general medical services and psychological treatment for a low cost. These services include consultations, a contraceptive advice clinic, eye screening, psychotherapy, physiotherapy, a discount pharmacy, and a confidential HIV-testing and counseling service. The HIV/AIDS unit is especially important at UCT because of the phenomenal AIDS rate in Africa. (In the year 2000, 22% of university undergraduates were infected with HIV.)

CAMPUS LIFE

The Student Representative Council (SRC) is very active and sponsors many clubs and events. This annually elected group of 15 students also provides a voice for the student body through its grievance advisory board, which helps students constructively criticize the administration. Students can even submit anonymous grievance forms on-line, which is a very helpful process at a university as large and as reportedly bureaucratic as UCT.

ADMISSIONS AND FINANCIAL INFO

Applications from international students are due by September 30 for the February semester and by April 15 for the July semester. Contact the international office for information on financial aid.

 CONTACTS

International Academic Programs Office
University of Cape Town
Private Bag
Rondebosch 7701
Republic of South Africa

Phone: 27-21-650-2822
Fax: 27-21-650-5667
E-mail: iapo@protem.uct.ac.za
URL: www.uct.ac.za

SPAIN

Saint Louis University, Madrid Campus

Madrid, Spain

AT A GLANCE

Founded in 1969 as a branch of the Jesuit Saint Louis University in Missouri, SLU Madrid is the first fully established American university campus in Spain. Students come here for the especially strong International Business, Marketing, and Economics majors, and of course for the chance to be at an American-accredited university in the fabulous city of Madrid.

Undergraduate Enrollment: 600; 200 Spanish, 200 American, 200 other nationalities
Male/Female: 55/45
Student/Faculty: 15/1
SAT Scores: 1165 average for entering freshmen
Tuition: $6,591 per semester
Accreditation: North Central Association of Colleges and Secondary Schools

CAMPUS AND LOCATION

SLU's Madrid campus is located on the northwest side of Madrid overlooking the Sierra de Guadarrama Mountains. The four buildings (two of which are restored eighteenth-century villas) that make up the main campus are all on one block in Madrid's university quarter. The area is teeming with students, many from the private Spanish university across the street, which allows SLU's international students the opportunity to interact with their Spanish peers. Madrid is Spain's capital city with a population of over three million. It is the political, cultural, and geographic heart of Spain. The city is also famous for its booming nightlife; in fact, most restaurants don't even open for dinner until about nine, and the streets are crowded until the wee hours of the morning.

ACADEMICS

Students seem to unanimously agree that at SLU academics are competitive and the level of class discourse is high, although they seem to be slightly at odds with the teaching style at SLU Madrid. While some felt that it was a great advantage to have mostly international teachers, one student mentioned that expectations were hard to predict—some professors graded by European standards, some by American standards. Regardless of their major, students must take a quarter of their classes in the arts, humanities, and sciences. One student complained about the core classes, saying, "In most classes students had a variety of different backgrounds and familiarity with the topics discussed. This made it impossible for the professor to advance the class without having to review basic topics." Field trips to historical sites around Western Europe are integrated into western civilization, philosophy, theology, and art classes. All degree-seeking students must also spend at least one year at SLU's St. Louis campus.

SPAIN

FACILITIES

Padre Arrupe Hall, a restored eighteenth-century mansion, contains the library, three computer labs, and biology, chemistry, and physics labs. The four computer labs on campus (one of which was recently donated by Hewlett-Packard Spain) are crowded at times, but boast the fastest internet connection in Spain and link the Madrid campus directly to the home campus in St. Louis. The on-campus bookstore provides bilingual textbooks and memorabilia as well as fax and copy services. The campus's small size seems to be a double-edged sword for students; while some feel that its compactness is an excellent social advantage, many also acknowledge that the lack of suitable recreational facilities makes it hard to hang out on campus. There are hopes that the recently enlarged café/snack bar will provide students with an outlet for socializing.

STUDENT HOUSING AND SERVICES

All freshmen are required to live in university-approved housing, although before arriving in Spain students with extenuating circumstances may petition for independent housing. The full room and board option, which includes three meals a day in the campus dining room, is available to only 30 men and 15 women. These catered facilities are located on campus and surrounded by small, private gardens. Each room has internet access, and both buildings provide laundry rooms, TV rooms, and common areas. Half room and board is available to women only. These accommodations are in three- to four-bedroom university-owned apartments about three blocks from campus. These flats have kitchens, internet access, and laundry facilities. Lunch (the main meal of the day in Spain) is provided in the campus dining room. A student may also participate in a homestay, which is a popular option. A list of host families from all around Madrid is available in the housing office, and students can choose to stay individually or with other students in one home.

Student services are limited at the small campus. Academic and social orientation is held at the beginning of fall semester and includes a three-day trip to either the Pyrenees or the Balearic Islands. The university provides students with a counseling service staffed by a professional, fully bilingual counselor and can also set students up with doctors in the area. The campus ministry promotes religious life at the university and provides information on worship around Madrid for all faiths. The ministry also organizes community service activities for interested students.

CAMPUS LIFE

SLU organizes cultural and recreational activities throughout the semester, including trips around Spain and museum tours with art history professors. The campus's many student associations also organize activities—for example, the Sierra Club sponsors weekend outdoor "adventures." Some other clubs include Shakespeare Aloud!, a literary club that hosts a monthly open-mike night at a local coffeehouse, a bilingual student newspaper and creative arts magazine, and a theater group that puts on two shows a year. The university offers elective classes in art and music, as well as traditional Spanish dancing classes for partial academic credit. It also organizes a choral group and private music instruction.

Madrid is a city with vast nightlife options. Off campus, students tend to congregate at the nearby Irish pubs. Capital, Joy, and Empire are all clubs popular with SLU students.

ADMISSIONS AND FINANCIAL INFO

Undergraduate degree-seeking students can apply on-line by March 30 for the fall semester and by October 15 for spring.

U.S. students may be eligible for financial aid from the St. Louis campus, as well as government grants. The Madrid campus also sponsors work grants, by which students work for 10 hours per week in exchange for a 15% reduction in tuition. Contact either campus for details.

CONTACTS

Saint Louis University Madrid Campus
Attn: Michelle LaBarge
Avda. Del Valle, 34
28003 Madrid,
Spain

Phone: 34-91-554-58-58
Fax: 34-91-554-62-02
E-mail: Madrid@spmail.slu.edu
URL: http://spain.slu.edu

U.S. Campus

Saint Louis University
Spain Program Office
221 North Grand Boulevard
St. Louis, MO 63103-2097

Phone: 314-968-7119
Toll-free: 800-984-6857
Fax: 314-968-7119
E-mail: admitme@slu.edu
URL: http://spain.slu.edu

Schiller International University, Madrid Campus

Madrid, Spain

AT A GLANCE

Schiller's Madrid campus does not rate as high academically with students as Schiller's other campuses, but it still offers a unique opportunity to study in one of the most exciting cities in Spain. (For more on SIU, see Schiller International University, Paris, page 125.)

> **Total Enrollment:** 170
> **Undergraduate Enrollment:** 150; 25% American, 25% E.U., 25% Spanish, 25% other nationalities
> **SAT Scores:** Not required
> **Tuition:** $11,995 per year
> **Accreditation:** Accrediting Council for Independent Colleges and Schools (ACICS)

CAMPUS AND LOCATION

SIU's Madrid campus is located in the Colomina Building in Argurelles, one of the prettiest neighborhoods in central Madrid. It is close to main shopping areas, cinemas, and theaters, and minutes away by subway or bus from the Old City and the Universidad Complutense de Madrid. The city of Madrid itself is home to many cities. There is the cultured city of museums, concerts, and theaters, and the traditional city of bullfights and festivals. The historical Madrid is home to many monuments, churches, convents, and palaces, with architecture of the Renaissance, Baroque, and Hapsburg periods. Then there is the modern Madrid, with its restaurants, nightclubs, and terrific party energy.

ACADEMICS

Aside from a few good professors here and there, students rate the academics at the Madrid campus as being pretty low. The degrees are thought to be very simple and straightforward, and one students said that if there is something that you want to learn, you are going to have to seek it out for yourself. SIU Madrid offers Associate Degrees in International Business, General Studies, and one year of the two-year Associate Degree program in International Hotel and Tourism Management with a concentration in Hotel Management. Students in this program take required and elective courses and participate in SIU's internship program. The college also offers a Bachelor of Business Administration degree with concentrations in Marketing and Management of Information Technology and Bachelor of Arts degrees in International Economics, International Relations and Diplomacy, and Interdepartmental Studies. Each program has specific core and language requirements.

FACILITIES

Aside from administrative offices and classrooms, the main campus building contains a student lounge, a snack bar, two computer rooms, a library, study rooms, and a career counseling office. Students have access to other libraries around Madrid, including the Biblioteca Nacional.

STUDENT HOUSING AND SERVICES

SIU Madrid doesn't offer campus residences. The college housing department keeps a current list of homestays and apartment rentals, but students complain that they feel pretty much left on their own in their search for good housing. There are also no official on-campus support services, but students say that at the small campus you can ask any faculty member to aid you. The admissions office also keeps a list of English-speaking doctors in the area.

CAMPUS LIFE

SIU Madrid organizes a variety of academic, cultural, and social activities. These are posted on the Activities Bulletin Board and the "Flash!" board in the student lounge. Some examples of previous events include an orientation party and neighborhood walking tours of Madrid, international dinners, and guest speakers from international companies.

ADMISSIONS AND FINANCIAL INFO

See Schiller International University, Paris, page 127.

CONTACTS

Schiller International University Madrid Campus
Offices San Bernardo 97-99 Edif. Colomina
28015 Madrid
Spain

Phone: 34-91-448-2488 ext.12
Fax: 34-91-593-4446
E-mail: admissions@schillermadrid.edu
URL: www.schillermadrid.edu

Continues ☞

U.S. Campus

Schiller International University
Florida Admissions Office and Central
  Administration Offices
453 Edgewater Drive
Dunedin, FL 34698-7532

Phone: 727-736-5082
Toll-free: 800-336-4133
Fax: 727-734-0359
E-mail: admissions@schiller.edu
URL: www.schiller.edu

SWITZERLAND

Franklin College

Lugano, Switzerland

AT A GLANCE

If you're in the market for a small American accredited liberal arts college with an academically committed student body in a beautiful European locale, then look no further. Franklin specializes in international relations, communications, and business, and it also offers a unique travel program that is included in the standard tuition as part of its core academic curriculum.

> **Undergraduate Enrollment:** 309; 45% American
> **Male/Female:** 42/58
> **Student/Faculty:** 10/1
> **SAT Scores:** 1160 average
> **Tuition:** $11,800 per semester
> **Accreditation:** The Commission on Higher Education of the Middle States Association of Colleges and Schools

CAMPUS AND LOCATION

Franklin College's main facilities are housed in a converted nineteenth-century villa situated on a hill above Lugano, a town on Switzerland's southernmost border. The Lake Lugano region, also known as the "Swiss Riviera," is lush and green with a Mediter-

Franklin College's grounds, nestled in
the picturesque Swiss Alps

ranean climate. With Italy right next door, it has an Italian atmosphere, and Italian is also the main language spoken in the region.
The rest of the college's nine buildings are located in the small village of Sorengo, about a 20-minute walk from the center of
Lugano. Lugano is a culturally rich town, with many museums, galleries, and concert halls. Students find the town's central location
(only an hour away from Milan) perfect for traveling throughout
the country and to other parts of Europe, but have some complaints
about the high cost of living in Switzerland. For more information
on the region, visit **www.lugano-tourism.com**.

ACADEMICS

Franklin students are reported to be very involved and serious about
academics. Starting freshman year, students follow a core curriculum in the liberal arts, which also includes the academic travel program, a unique aspect of Franklin's truly multicultural education. In
this program, students must complete six two-week professor-led

trips to destinations around the world in conjunction with a short related seminar. Throughout the travel program, students work on a number of short assignments, culminating in a final paper. These travel programs are taken for one credit each, and the travel costs (transportation, accommodation, and meals) are included in the price of tuition. Students remarked that these "amazing" experiences were like "getting to take a new study abroad program every year!" Some spring 2001 travel programs included studying ancient civilization in Rome and Pompeii; impressionism in England; the origins of mankind in Namibia; Russia's artistic heritage in Moscow and St. Petersburg; and art, culture, and politics in Cuba.

FACILITIES

One of the only complaints about Franklin is the size of the campus. Many students feel that the cozy villa is just too small to accommodate what amounts to almost all of the main academic facilities, including the David R. Grace library, reading rooms, computer labs, and classrooms. (A separate building nearby houses art studios and facilities.) On-campus athletic facilities include the Leonardo da Vinci Gym, a fitness room, and a soccer field. The college also has an agreement with local fitness clubs to provide discounted memberships to students.

STUDENT HOUSING AND SERVICES

For such a small school, Franklin offers a large volume of housing. All freshmen and sophomores are required to live on campus, and 82% of upperclassmen chose to remain in college housing through graduation. Franklin's eight residence halls are all a few blocks from the main building and have live-in resident advisors. The residences offer fully furnished self-catered singles, suites, and doubles. Meal plans are available for an extra charge.

The Student Services office assists students in all aspects of college life. The office and the Dean of Students coordinate health and counseling services at the school infirmary and with a licensed therapist, and help students set up residency permits and health insurance.

CAMPUS LIFE

The office of student affairs organizes a number of extracurricular activities for interested students. The fall semester kicks off with International Food Night, a culinary competition giving new students a chance to represent their national identities. There is a winter and spring formal and a Thanksgiving dinner prepared by students and faculty. Every Sunday is movie night in the auditorium, and there are a number of student clubs, including a Latin American club, an Arabic club, a ski club, a photo club, a drama society, a culinary club, an athletics club, and a soccer team.

ADMISSIONS AND FINANCIAL INFO

Franklin operates on a rolling admissions policy. A number of scholarships are offered each year, such as the Franklin Scholar Award, consisting of $10,000 and a laptop, given to eligible freshmen, and the Ben Franklin award, a $6,000 scholarship given to four students who have a strong interest in cross-cultural studies and communications.

 CONTACTS

Franklin College
via Ponte Tresa 29
6924 Sorengo (Lugano)
Switzerland

Phone: 41-91-985-22-60
Fax: 41-91-994-41-17
E-mail: info@fc.edu
URL: www.fc.edu

Continues ☞

U.S. Office

Franklin College
91-31 Queens Boulevard, Suite 411
Elmhurst, NY 11373

Phone: 718-335-6800
Fax: 718-335-6733

Schiller International University, Leysin Campus

Leysin, Switzerland

AT A GLANCE

In 1994 Schiller bought the American College of Switzerland, a small two-year international college in a historic resort hotel, to house its Leysin campus. Students come for the gorgeous location in the French Alps as well as for the strong Bachelor of Arts program. (For more on SIU see Schiller International University, Paris, page 125.)

Total Enrollment: 100
SAT Scores: Not required
Tuition: $7,536 per year
Accreditation: Accrediting Council for Independent
   Colleges and Schools

CAMPUS AND LOCATION

The Leysin campus at the American College of Switzerland (ACS) is housed in the modernized Victorian "Grand Hotel" complex on an 11-acre campus, complete with its own train and bus stations. The Grand Hotel was built in 1892 and is located in the Vaudoise Alps overlooking the lovely village and ski resort of Leysin. (*The Magic Mountain,* a film based on Thomas Mann's novel, was filmed at the Grand Hotel in 1980.)

The resort town of Leysin is located on the eastern end of Lake Geneva, close to the larger towns of Montreux, Lausanne, and Geneva. Once a small farming community, the area is now a very popular ski destination, with many chalets (as well as tourists), restaurants, a movie theater, shopping areas, and two indoor sports centers.

ACADEMICS

SIU Leysin offers Associate of Arts, Bachelor of Business Administration, Bachelor of Science, and Bachelor of Arts degrees. Minors and various concentrations are available within the degree programs, and students must complete the General Core program (except for the Bachelor of Arts, Interdepartmental Studies Major). The college also offers a one-year diploma program in international business.

SIU students are encouraged to apply for internships with international and governmental organizations. In the past, students have been placed at the United Nations Center for Human Rights, the International Labor Office, CIBA-GEIGY, Paine Webber, and Cargill International in Geneva.

FACILITIES

The ACS library, housed in the four-story La Pyrole, is one of the largest English libraries in Switzerland, and the college also participates in the Swiss Inter-Library Loan program. SIU's new reading room with internet access is located in the main college building next to the bookstore. The Grand Hotel houses classrooms, faculty offices, language and computer labs, a darkroom, lounges, a grand salon, a student snack bar, a TV room, and a dining hall. It is also the home of the conference center, which offers 136 guest rooms, a cafeteria, the Belle Epoque ballroom, and a bar that opens onto a garden with a disco, a digital satellite TV, a pool, and Ping-Pong tables.

STUDENT HOUSING AND SERVICES

Campus housing is available for up to 250 students in the Grand Hotel. Most rooms are double occupancy with their own bathrooms, but, for a fee, some single rooms may be available. Resident advisors live in the residence halls, and laundry facilities are available.

SIU provides its new students with an orientation featuring social events and excursions. Academic and personal counseling is available, and all SIU students have access to career counseling and internship placement. There are no campus health services, but students are referred to the two doctors in town (both of whom speak English).

CAMPUS LIFE

The Cave is the SIU Leysin student center and hub of campus social life. It serves as a café, club, and entertainment center, with movies, a satellite TV, and a game room.

The campus organizes a Distinguished Speakers series that features visiting lecturers and also conducts current events workshops with members of the international business community.

ADMISSIONS AND FINANCIAL INFO

See Schiller International University, Paris, page 127.

CONTACTS

Admissions Office
Schiller International University
The American College of Switzerland
CH-1854 Leysin
Switzerland

Phone: 41-24-493-0309
Fax: 41-24-493-0300
E-mail: siuacsadmissions@bluewin.ch
URL: www.american-college.com

U.S. Campus

Schiller International University
Florida Admissions Office and Central
  Administration Offices
453 Edgewater Drive
Dunedin, FL 34698-7532

Phone: 727-736-5082
Toll-free: 800-336-4133
Fax: 727-734-0359
E-mail: admissions@schiller.edu
URL: www.schiller.edu

THAILAND

Webster University Thailand

Cha-am, Thailand

AT A GLANCE

If you've ever dreamed of studying business in a beautiful Asian paradise, then Webster Thailand just might be the school for you. Opened in 1999, it is the youngest in Webster's network of international campuses. The gorgeous campus offers Webster's standard preprofessional degree programs, as well as a number of Thailand-specific courses, all taught in a community-oriented environment. (For more on Webster University, see Webster University Netherlands, page 208.)

Total Enrollment: 262; 21% American, 18% Vietnamese, 11% Burmese, 10% Indian, 10% Nepalese
Undergraduate Enrollment: 203
Male/Female: 41/59
Student/Faculty: 11/1
SAT Scores: 1100 required
Tuition: $8,080 per year
Accreditation: North Central Association of Colleges and Schools

---

THAILAND

CAMPUS AND LOCATION

Webster Thailand's main facilities are housed in a brand-new 30-acre lush campus about 140 miles southwest of Bangkok near the very wealthy towns of Cha-am and Hua Hin. This popular resort area is home to the summer palace of the king of Thailand, and features many five-star hotels and some of the best golf courses in Asia. The towns are very safe and well-maintained.

Students looking for more variety can head to Bangkok, about two hours away from the main campus. The city is an interesting mix of eastern tradition and western capitalism. You are as likely to see Buddhist monks collecting their morning alms as you are to see a Baskin-Robbins or Blockbuster Video. You can even check out Bangkok's fully functional ancient marketplace as you ride high above on the city's new Skytrain, an elevated public transportation system.

ACADEMICS

Webster's undergraduate programs are designed to give students a competitive edge in the job market. The university offers similar degree programs at all campuses in Advertising and Marketing, Communications, Media Communications, Psychology, Business Administration, Computer Science, International Business and Management, and Marketing. Most classes are taught by professionals in their field, and students are encouraged to participate in internship programs. The mandatory General Education Curriculum provides all students with a well-rounded liberal arts background. As part of the broad curriculum, students at the Thailand campus are offered a whole range of courses relating to Thai culture and language, as well as a special Buddhism program.

FACILITIES

Webster Thailand features some of the most extensive facilities of any of the university's overseas campuses. The campus is comprised of a three-story administration building with a separate two-story library, a general computer and media lab, two labs for IT students, and a separate psychology lab. Recreational facilities include tennis courts and a large gym, faculty and student lounges with cable TV, and a prayer room for Muslim students. The cafeteria with its landscaped open-air patio serves a number of different types of international cuisine.

STUDENT HOUSING AND SERVICES

Students are housed in two residences about 20 minutes away from campus in luxurious (at least by dorm standards) accommodations by the beach. A shuttle bus runs until 9 P.M. to connect the residences to the campus. One residence is a hotel with air-conditioned rooms that have cable TV and face a central swimming pool. The other residence features balconied condo-style accommodations with similar amenities to the hotel. Housing costs are just $850 per year. There is no meal plan, but a multicourse meal in the cafeteria will only set you back about $1.

Academic counseling and orientation activities are provided by the Department of Student Services, and psychological counseling is provided by a professor of psychology. The campus recently opened a health clinic run by the local hospital.

CAMPUS LIFE

Students report that there is a strong sense of community on campus, and with such a a large number of resources, there are many ways to get involved in extracurricular activities. The student council organizes events throughout the year, and there is a student newspaper (*WUT News*) and cricket and football teams. Pretty much anyone can start up a club, and with the strong student-teacher rapport, many professors roll up their sleeves and join in too, like the drama professor who organizes the WUT players, directing them in about four productions a year, or the professor who recently brought students down to the beach for a clean-up day and impromptu sand castle contest. The university organizes visits to temples and historical sites and sponsors social awareness programs.

Off campus, students can live it up in Cha-am and Hua Hin. Although these towns are small, the booming tourism industry has ensured that there are many international restaurants, nightclubs, bars, and other ways to keep amused. To catch up on their conspicuous consumption, students head to Bangkok's Siam Square, a huge mall complex that provides many a weekend's diversion with its huge video game arcades, multiplex theaters, and stores that you'd find in the mall at home, like The Gap and Armani Exchange.

ADMISSIONS AND FINANCIAL INFO

Specific enquiries can be directed to the Bangkok office. Otherwise see Webster University Netherlands, page 211.

 CONTACTS

Webster University
Information Center
518/5 Box 40 Maneeya Center, 7th Floor
Ploenchit Road
Bangkok, 10330
Thailand

Tel: 66-2-652-0705
Fax: 66-2-652-0708
E-mail: wuthai@loxinfo.co.th
URL: www.webster.edu/thailand

Continues ☞

U.S. Office

Webster University
Office of Undergraduate Admissions
470 East Lockwood Avenue
St. Louis, MO 63119-3194
Phone: 314-968-6991
Toll-free: 1-800-75-ENROLL
Fax: 314-968-7115

TURKEY

Girne American University

Northern Cyprus, Turkey

AT A GLANCE

Girne American University was founded in 1985 as an American-accredited business-oriented college in a beautiful small Mediterranean town. The university caters to a primarily Turkish student body with a handful of visiting American students each semester.

Total Enrollment: 2,000
Undergraduate Enrollment: 1,700; 18% international
Male/Female: 58/42
Student/Faculty: 11/1
SAT Scores: Not required
Tuition: $5,250 per year
Accreditation: International Assembly for Collegiate Business Education (IACBE, the prime accrediting body for specialist business colleges and schools in the U.S.), European Council of International Schools (ECIS) member

CAMPUS AND LOCATION

GAU's campus lies on a plateau overlooking the Mediterranean sea and is nestled under the Beşparmak (or "Five Fingers") mountain range in the Turkish Republic of Northern Cyprus, about 40 miles off the southern coast of Turkey. The small campus's landscaped gardens and fountains surround the modern main academic buildings. GAU's campus is on the outskirts of the village of Karaoglanoglu, where students can shop and explore the ancient and picturesque fishing harbor, or stop in one of the many bars or restaurants.

ACADEMICS

Undergraduate degrees are taught across four faculties: Education, Business and Economics, Engineering and Architecture, and Law. At the beginning of freshman year, students must declare a major although they can change it with the Faculty Dean's approval.

Students may also be eligible to participate in ten-week internship programs organized and supervised by a faculty member.

FACILITIES

The main academic building houses the library and computer labs, dining hall, bookshop, gym, cinema, and conference room. Other campus facilities include basketball and tennis courts and architectural and multimedia studios.

STUDENT HOUSING AND SERVICES

Students are housed in small one- or two-bedroom apartments in hostels in Girne, a few miles away from the main campus. A regular shuttle service connects the dorms to the university. Students can also chose to participate in homestays.

Because of its small size, the university offers limited services. Upon enrollment, students are assigned an academic advisor from their department who helps them with all school-related issues.

GAU also offers personal counseling. There is a small infirmary on campus that can handle minor emergencies, but in more serious cases, students have access to the nearby Girne State Hospital.

CAMPUS LIFE

The student union at GAU organizes many social, cultural, and sports clubs like scuba diving and billiards. It also has a student-run radio station and publishes *GAU Online,* the student newspaper. (You can read it on the university's web site at **www.gau.edu.tr**.)

ADMISSIONS AND FINANCIAL INFO

Admissions operate on a rolling basis. Space permitting, students may apply up to one week before the start of the academic year. Students who have completed one year of undergraduate study with a GPA of at least 3.0 may be eligible for academic scholarships.

 CONTACTS

Girne American University
Office of Admission
Karmi Campus
P.O. Box 5, Girne
North Cyprus via Mersin 10
Turkey

Phone: 90-392-822-3203
Fax: 90-392-822-2403
E-mail: gau@gau.edu.tr or admissions@gau.edu.tr
URL: www.gau.edu.tr

THE UNITED KINGDOM AND THE REPUBLIC OF IRELAND

The U.K. does things a bit differently when it comes to higher education. For starters (as we mentioned in the introduction) a university education in the U.K. is very specialized. You must decide what you want to major in when you apply, and generally you cannot change your mind. Another main difference is in the way courses are assessed. At many universities, class attendance is *not* mandatory, and sometimes classes are *only* assessed through exams at the end of a term. Students in the U.K. are also generally better educated than their American peers. This means that regular American high school qualifications (i.e., a diploma and SAT scores) are not enough to get you into many universities in the U.K. Sometimes U.S. applicants are required to have a year of college under their belts, but generally you can squeak by as long as you have scores of 4 or higher on a number of AP tests.

Introducing UCAS

Most universities in the U.K. have one thing in common: the Universities and Colleges Admissions Service, or UCAS, a centralized application processing organization for almost all universities and colleges in the U.K. Most Americans have never heard of UCAS, but for students in the U.K., it's a way of life.

What exactly is UCAS and how does it work?

Students from all over the world use the UCAS form to apply directly to up to six programs or faculties of colleges and universities at once (the underlying concept being that you're not applying to a university but to a specific course). Filling out the application can be as confusing as hell. We recommend that you enlist the aid of a college counselor or your local British Council representative (who has to provide you with the form anyway).

Once the application has been sent in, you wait. When UCAS has received all your application materials, it contacts the universities. Then the universities contact UCAS to let them know if you are accepted, and then UCAS contacts you. Throughout this time, you may be asked to submit additional information, depending on what programs you have applied to. UCAS is purely an intermediary and plays no role in making admissions decisions. Each university has its own requirements and may also require international students to submit an application to supplement the UCAS form. If you do not receive any offers from your chosen programs, you become eligible for "Clearing," whereby you can apply to other courses that still have vacancies, including courses at universities you have already applied to.

Some Important Dates

September 1: First date applications can be sent.
October 15: Applications for Oxford, Cambridge, and medical programs due.
March 24: Applications for Art and Design Route "B" programs due.
June 30: All other applications from outside the E.U. due.
September 20: Applications for Clearing due.

Here are some terms you can use to impress your new U.K. friends:

- A-Levels: the top secondary school qualifications in the U.K. system.
- Catered: residence halls with dining facilities.
- Honors/joint honors degree: an undergraduate degree usually including an extra year of study, sort of like an American master's program (lasting a total of four years, as opposed to the three-year regular degree). A joint honors degree allows you to specialize in two subjects.
- Residential colleges: Many universities in the U.K. are broken up into smaller residential colleges, which means that you live, take classes, and socialize in the same buildings.
- Residence halls: traditional dorms.
- Self-catered: a residence with cooking facilities.
- Tutorial: a small or private class, similar to an American seminar, but often a bit more in-depth, depending on the university.

 CONTACTS

UCAS Application Requests
Rosehill
New Barn Lane
Cheltenham
Gloucestershire
GL52 3LZ
England

Phone: 44-870-112-2211
Fax: 44-124-254-4961
E-mail: app.req@ucas.ac.uk
URL: www.ucas.com

Continues ☞

> **The British Council**
> The British Embassy
> 3100 Massachusetts Avenue, NW
> Washington, D.C. 20008-3600
>
> **Phone:** 202-588-6500
> **Toll-free:** 800-488-2235
> **Fax:** 202-588-7918
>
> Visit their web site for an amazingly comprehensive guide to studying in the U.K. at **www.britishcouncil-usa.org.**

American College Dublin

Dublin, Ireland

AT A GLANCE

Although its name may imply otherwise, American College Dublin is not actually accredited in the United States. This small and personable international college with strong business and management courses offers an American-inspired liberal arts core curriculum, as well as an exchange program with the Lynn University in Boca Raton, Florida.

> **Undergraduate Enrollment:** 450; 16% American, 45% other nationalities
> **Male/Female:** 52/48
> **Student/Faculty:** 20/1
> **SAT Scores:** 1000 required
> **Tuition:** $7,427 per year
> **Accreditation:** In Ireland through the National Council for Educational Awards

CAMPUS AND LOCATION

American College Dublin was founded in 1993 as an educational trust by Lynn University. ACD's city campus consists of three large restored Georgian townhouses, one of which was actually the childhood home of Oscar Wilde and is now the Oscar Wilde House Museum. The campus is located in Merrion Square in the center of Dublin, the capital of the Republic of Ireland. Dublin has a rich cultural and literary tradition and has been home to such greats as Jonathan Swift, George Bernard Shaw, W.B. Yeats, James Joyce, and Samuel Beckett. With three universities, Dublin is also a major student town with a very young population.

ACADEMICS

ACD offers degree and diploma programs in International Business (Management or Marketing), Hospitality Management, and Behavioral Science (Psychology or Applied Social Studies). Students take six classes a semester, which are generally small and discussion-oriented. Students in all programs must follow a core curriculum of liberal arts subjects designed to give them a foundation in human behavior studies as well as practical skills like writing, public speaking, and languages. Most programs also require students to participate in an internship with one of the many Irish or international companies that have relationships with the college. Students can also study abroad at a number of destinations through an exchange with Lynn University (**www.lynn.edu**).

FACILITIES

ACD's Rooney Library houses relevant books, periodicals, and electronic resources, and is also linked to the library system at Lynn University, giving students access to another 11 million volumes. There is a general computer lab on campus as well as a specialized psychology computer lab. A language lab offers courses and has resources for students working on their own.

STUDENT HOUSING AND SERVICES

International students are housed in the international residence hall located on Lower Mount Street a few minutes from the campus in a building resembling a Holiday Inn (in a good, clean sort of way). Students are accommodated in single, double, or triple rooms, all with basic furnishings, as well as phones and internet access. The residence hall has 24-hour security at the reception desk and special facilities such as a study room, a computer lab, a gym and exercise room, a TV room, and a game room. Breakfast and dinner are served daily in the dining room, and there is a student affairs office in the building to assist students. Fees for the residence hall are about $6,240 per year. The student housing office can also help students arrange homestays with Irish families for about $200 per week.

Support services are a bit limited. International students have their own advisor and an orientation at the beginning of the year; otherwise, the dean of students and his office are available at all times to help with student welfare issues.

CAMPUS LIFE

ACD's small international student body is an active one. Its student council is elected annually and is responsible for organizing extracurricular activities on campus. There are also a number of active student clubs, such as the drama group, which produces at least one major production per semester. Sports play a big role in campus life—ACD's soccer team has already begun to make a name for itself in the Division B Irish Technical Colleges' Football Association league, and the basketball team won the Division B Irish Colleges' Basketball Association league championship in 1997.

Between classes, students enjoy hanging out at Speranza's, the student café, which serves food and drink during the day and has a TV room and lounge.

ADMISSIONS AND FINANCIAL INFO

American students are required to have finished high school and must submit relevant standardized test scores. Admissions operate on a rolling basis until the start of the semester. ACD does not offer any financial aid.

 CONTACTS

American College Dublin
2 Merrion Square
Dublin 2
Ireland

Phone: 353-1-676-8939
Fax: 353-1-676-8941
E-mail: degree@amcd.ie
URL: www.amcd.ie

British American College London at Regent's College

London, England

AT A GLANCE

British American College London is a very small college, although a new web site and more active recruiting practices have increased its number of applicants by 250% in the past two years. It offers an American degree through a partnership with Webster College in St. Louis. (For more on Webster see page 237.) BACL is also known for its business programs and very international student body.

> **Undergraduate Enrollment:** 400; 19% E.U.,
>   17% American, 16% Middle Eastern, 10% U.K.
> **SAT Scores:** 1100 required
> **Tuition:** $14,600 per year
> **Accreditation:** North Central Association Commission on
>   Institutions of Higher Education through Webster College
>   in St. Louis

CAMPUS AND LOCATION

BACL is located on the campus of Regent's College, which was built in 1913 and is surrounded by lawns, gardens, and tennis courts. Although the campus is green and peaceful, it is still in the heart of bustling London, close to the Baker Street tube station. Regent's College shares its campus not only with BACL, but also with the European Business School London, Regents Business School

London, Regents International Study Center London, the School of Psychotherapy and Counseling, and Webster Graduate Studies Center.

ACADEMICS

BACL's American undergraduate degree provides a well-rounded liberal arts education. The 128 credits (each class is worth three credits) required for a degree are made up of four elements—the major, general education requirements, the minor (optional), and electives. First-year students must follow the Freshman Year Plan in which they choose a possible major and their academic advisor helps them choose other relevant courses. The FYP is designed to introduce students to their major and help them complete some general education requirements. The FYP consists of two courses in a major area and three courses in general education/study skills— writing, math, and computing. BACL is good at bridging the gap between the classroom and practical experience. Its business programs are particularly strong and many professors have managerial experience at international companies. One German student said that he chose BACL because "The electives are much more practical, and [classes are] up-to-date with the newest theories and trends in management."

Internship programs are available to upperclassmen for credit. Previous placements have been at the Bayswater Homeless Center, the London Zoo, NBC, Fairchild Publishing, the Soho Theater, and the Greater London Labor Party. Students can also take advantage of BACL's exchange programs with over 40 U.S. universities, including Skidmore, Tulane, and Long Island University. Students may also be able to audit some classes at Regent's College at the individual professor's discretion.

FACILITIES

BACL essentially has access to the facilities of all five colleges at Regent's. The Tate Library houses books, journals, periodicals, dissertations, videos, and DVDs, and it offers students satellite TV services, video viewing rooms, copy machines, and PCs with internet access. The campus's information technology center has 225 PCs and Macs, as well as teaching rooms with computer presentation facilities. The college also has a bookshop, a student bar (which features a big-screen TV, a pool table, and video games), and a recently opened internet café. The campus has its own tennis and basketball courts as well as a small fitness center with a sauna and a dance studio.

STUDENT HOUSING AND SERVICES

Reid Hall, a gorgeous ivy-covered building, accommodates 220 students (mostly Americans) in single, double, and triple rooms. Stu-

A bird's-eye view of
Regent's campus, home to
the British American College London

dents report that the best thing about this residence is its beautiful views overlooking the surrounding lake and park, and its security—a college guard is stationed at the front desk 24/7. Another housing facility, Oliver Hall, is much smaller with only 12 doubles. Housing includes meals at the refectory, so neither dorm has kitchen facilities. Students are allowed to have refrigerators in their rooms (but not microwaves or hot plates).

Academic counseling is available through the student advisors and also through student services, which arranges professional counseling outside the school and helps students register with a local National Health Service doctor. Students living on campus can receive free treatment at the campus health center.

CAMPUS LIFE

BACL's student center can help new students get the most out of their college experience in London. It throws parties and karaoke nights and also provides students with music practice rooms. It also organizes bargain tickets to shows and guided city tours and weekend trips in the area. Regent's College has intramural football, volleyball, and basketball teams open to BACL students.

ADMISSIONS AND FINANCIAL INFO

Applicants are required to have a 2.5 GPA, two letters of recommendation, and a personal statement. BACL offers a number of merit scholarships worth up to half the total tuition fees per semester, as well as a media communications scholarship for students with strong achievement in that area. The winner of this grant receives half off tuition and assumes editorial responsibility for the campus journal. Some work-study jobs are available, but they are awarded based on academic merit. Students wishing to be considered for grants must include a statement in their application of what contributions they would make to their college community.

CONTACTS

Ms. Erin McGuigan
Senior Admissions and Business Development Officer
External Relations
British American College London
Regent's College
Regent's Park
London NW1 4NS
England

Phone: 44-20-7487-7452
Fax: 44-20-7487-7425
E-mail: mcguigae@regents.ac.uk
URL: www.bacl.ac.uk

Central Saint Martins College of Art and Design
London, England

AT A GLANCE

This internationally renowned college is one of the most distinguished art and design schools in the world, and offers some of the most diverse and comprehensive courses in art, design and communications in the U.K. Central Saint Martins is a specialist college of the London Institute (**www.linst.ac.uk**), which also encompasses Camberwell College of Arts, London College of Printing, Chelsea College of Art and Design, and London College of Fashion.

Total Enrollment: 3,500
Undergraduate Enrollment: 2,500
Male/Female: 35/65
Tuition: $11,554 per year
SAT Scores: Not required
Accreditation: Degrees awarded by the London Institute

CAMPUS AND LOCATION

Central Saint Martins College of Art and Design (also known as Central Saint Martins or Saint Martins College) was formed in 1989 when the Central School of Art and Design merged with the Saint Martins School of Art. In 1999, the college formed another merger, this time with the Drama Center London, and has since incorporated performing arts programs into its repertoire.

Central Saint Martins is based in central London, with other buildings in Charing Cross Road, Hoborn, Clerkenwell, and Camden.

ACADEMICS

Central Saint Martins offers career-oriented degrees in the fields of Fine Art, Fashion and Textiles, Graphics and Communication Design, Three-dimensional Design, Theater and Performance, and Interdisciplinary Art and Design. Many courses emphasize the professional side of the arts and organize class projects with private clients in the art and design sector. All students must take the Foundation Studies course, which introduces them to a whole range of subjects, before they decide on a future specialization. The course also gives students the strong arts base they need for any career in art and design. Although all of Central Saint Martins programs are strong, the college is especially reputable in the field of fashion. In 1998, it was awarded the Queen's Anniversary Prize to mark its contribution to the development of the fashion industry, and the college's alumni include some of the biggest names in recent fashion history, such as John Galliano, Alexander McQueen, and Stella McCartney.

FACILITIES

It's probably not an overstatement to say that Central Saint Martins has every imaginable type of facility needed to produce professional-quality art and design work. Many specialized multimedia and general computer labs are available around campus, and there are workshops and studios provided for all mediums. The Charing Cross Road campus has a fine art and fashion library. The slide library and a general library for all other disciplines are located at Southampton Row. Students have access to all other libraries in the London Institute, a consortium of art colleges of which Central Saint Martins is a member. The Lethaby Gallery and Cochrane Theatre are large venues for student, staff, and alumni works. The college also has on-campus dining facilities, a bar, and an art supply store.

HOUSING AND STUDENT SERVICES

Students are housed in halls of residence at the London Institute. Priority for on-campus housing is given to first-year and international students. The London Institute also has a housing service to assist students who have been unsuccessful in getting a place at one of the halls or who simply wish to find privately rented accommodation. The London Institute student services offers support to people with disabilities and has an international students coordinator, a professional counseling and health care service, a careers service, and a nursery.

CAMPUS LIFE

Like most schools in big cities, Central Saint Martins does not have an especially college-y vibe. Students here are serious about their work and into doing their own thing. That being said, the London Institute, of which Saint Martins is a member, does offer a number of sports organizations and cultural, religious, artistic, and entertainment societies, as well as ways to get involved in the community through community service and fund-raising activities. To learn more, visit the London Institute's student union web site at **www.lisu.org.**

ADMISSIONS AND FINANCIAL INFO

For all courses except B.A. Fashion—History and Theory and B.A. Acting, apply to UCAS on Route B by March 24.

For B.A. Fashion—History and Theory, apply to UCAS either on Route A or Route B.

For B.A. Acting, apply to UCAS on Route A by May 15 for the fall term and by October 15 for the spring term. (For more information on UCAS, see page 245.)

All applicants must submit a portfolio with their application forms, except for B.A. (Honors) Fashion—History and Theory and B.A. (Honors) Acting. Specific advice on what to include in your portfolio is included in each course listing on the web site. American students are not eligible for any scholarships or financial aid.

 CONTACTS

Central Saint Martins
Information Office
Southampton Row
London WC1B 4AP
England

Phone: 44-20-7514-7022
Fax: 44-20-7514-7254
E-mail: info@csm.linst.ac.uk
URL: www.csm.linst.ac.uk

International Office

Phone: 44-20-7514-7027
Fax: 44-20-7514-8013
E-mail: international-office@csm.linst.ac.uk

Goldsmiths College

London, England

AT A GLANCE

Goldsmiths College is a relatively small college in the University of London system, with a reputation for being arty and alternative. Some famous alumni include the artists Lucien Freud and Damian Hirst and the designer Mary Quant. One student had this to say about his Goldsmiths experience: "Modern facilities, progressive language learning techniques, a helpful and friendly team of staff, a trendy image, open-mindedness, and the best student union events in town. This is what I found just in my first term here."

Total Enrollment: 8,339; 1,087 international
Undergraduate Enrollment: 5,255
Male/Female: 44/66
Student/Faculty: 16/1
SAT Scores: Not required
Tuition: $20,806–$23,200 per year

CAMPUS AND LOCATION

Goldsmiths College was officially established in 1904 but was not incorporated into the University of London until 1989. Goldsmiths is located in New Cross, in the Borough of Lewisham in South East London, close to the Thames waterfront at Greenwich. It is about 20 minutes from central London by train. South East London is vibrant, bursting at the seams with history and culture. There's a large variety of places to eat and drink in Greenwich, Blackheath,

Brixton, and Camberwell. Around New Cross there are cafés, pubs, "takeaways," and restaurants, as well as a newly opened giant Sainsbury supermarket. But be aware that New Cross is actually a somewhat dangerous part of town: one student said, "Bad points have to be the fact that the 'Annual Muggers Convention' seems to meet here every day. But, all in all, it's well worth it."

ACADEMICS

Although Goldsmiths offers three-year degrees in a wide range of subjects (mostly in humanities, the arts, and social sciences) its strengths lie in its art classes, which students describe as being "amazing." This is not to say that other subjects are not strong. One of the unique aspects of a Goldsmiths education (as opposed to other "art" schools) is that students studying art have the benefit of being in an intellectual environment, and students from other disciplines benefit from the creative opportunities on campus. Classes are taught through seminar discussions, about which one student said, "The support and encouragement received from fellow students and tutors is a great confidence-booster, enabling even the most reticent to air their views in an academic environment."

In their third year, students are able to choose subjects from a broad range of study areas and also work on dissertations. Students report that it takes a bit more motivation to succeed at Goldsmiths. Said one, "It truly required a lot of self-control to actually do the reading and attend lectures where they didn't take attendance."

FACILITIES

The award-winning Rutherford Information Services Building houses the library, computer labs, the language resource center, media services, and the copy center. Goldsmiths library is one of London's best for social, cultural, and media studies, with a large multimedia collection. Media and AV services offer digital video and 35mm cameras and projectors, digital video editing, and other AV equipment. Student facilities also include campus sports fields and the Loring Sports Ground, off campus but nearby.

STUDENT HOUSING AND SERVICES

All new students are guaranteed on-campus housing their first year, and all non-E.U. students are guaranteed housing throughout their degree program. Goldsmiths offers accommodations for over 1,030 students within walking distance of campus. Over 750 rooms have their own in-suite bathrooms. The accommodation office tries to make sure each hall has a good mix of students from different degrees and at various stages of study, so students can make friends from across the academic community. Of course, this doesn't always work. One American study abroad student in her junior year complained that she was housed with freshmen, and that "none of my British flatmates wanted to be friends with Americans."

Goldsmiths offers a range of student support services, covering financial and academic support. The college's careers services office is part of the University of London careers services, the largest in the U.K. It offers talks and seminars and recently launched a career web site. On-campus representatives of Christian and Jewish faiths help with students' spiritual needs, and the medical center provides physical and mental care, as well as an overseas travel health advice clinic.

CAMPUS LIFE

Students find Goldsmiths' relatively small campus a lively, welcoming place with a lot going on. Goldsmiths has its own student union, which offers "fun concerts and cheap pints," and students also have access to the huge University of London student union. Because Goldsmiths has such a strong reputation for the arts, the student body tends to be arty. On the flip side, some students say that there is a fair amount of drug activity on campus. Some study abroad students felt that there was not much attempt made by the administration to integrate them into the rest of the student body. But others disagree. Said one, "Socially, I found a friendly community spirit. The compact nature of the college means that there is ample chance to meet people, while the student union provides the opportunity to party at least once a week!"

ADMISSIONS AND FINANCIAL INFO

Admission to Goldsmiths is fairly competitive. Students with American high school credentials must also have two AP tests with a score of at least 3 in subjects related to their chosen course of study. Contact the International Office for more details and specific course requirements. Apply through UCAS (see page 245).

 CONTACTS

International Office
Goldsmiths College
University of London
New Cross
London SE14 6NW
England

Phone: 44-20-7919-7700
Fax: 44-20-7919-7704
E-mail: international-office@gold.ac.uk
URL: www.goldsmiths.ac.uk

King's College London

London, England

AT A GLANCE

A very respected college in the University of London system, King's offers students a flexible education with a great location in central

London, and a purportedly "lighthearted and bubbly" student body.

Total Enrollment: 17,000
Undergraduate Enrollment: 12,400
SAT Scores: Required, but minimum depends on faculty
Tuition: $14,104–$17,550 per year

CAMPUS AND LOCATION

Founded in 1829 by King George IV and the Duke of Wellington, King's College is one of the oldest colleges in the University of London system. King's four campuses are located along the Thames in central London. The college also has a fifth campus in South London, reachable by shuttle. King's Strand campus (its humanities main base) is thought by students to be its best campus.

ACADEMICS

King's offers degrees in over 200 undergraduate programs across its nine schools: Biomedical Sciences, Dentistry, Health and Life Sciences, Humanities, Law, Medicine, Nursing and Midwifery, Physical Sciences and Engineering, and Social Sciences and Public Policy.

King's encourages interdisciplinary learning through its unique Associateship of King's College program, a group of noncredit courses available to students in all departments. In the Associateship, students attend a series of open academic lectures once a week for an hour that cover morality, medical ethics, philosophy, theology, and biblical studies. Although these courses are not required, and are reportedly very easy to pass, one law student said that she felt they were "invaluable in the way that they broaden your horizons," and that they allowed her to explore areas she would have otherwise been unable to in her major. The study of languages is also encouraged at King's. The modern language center offers for-credit and free extracurricular courses (for non–language majors) to students as well as a self-learning facility with satellite TV, language software, and other media tools. For students who need a change of scenery, King's College participates in study abroad exchanges with over 50 European universities.

FACILITIES

The five floors of King's Macadam building house the advice center and the Lion's Walk, a commercial floor featuring a union shop, STA travel, a bookstore, an insurance center, and Barclay's bank. The building also features a deli, fitness facilities, a café, a bar, and a nightclub. King's Guy's campus, which recently underwent a £1 million renovation, has another union shop, a nightclub, a bookstore, and a coffee lounge, as well as a gym with a swimming pool. King's Denmark Hill and St. Thomas's campuses have bars and dining facilities. Each campus has library facilities and computer labs. The brand-new Chauncery Lane Humanities Library is supposedly the nicest at King's. Most campus computer facilities are open 24 hours a day.

STUDENT HOUSING AND SERVICES

Housing priority is given to non-U.K. students. Most of King's residences are in central London and are comprised of catered and self-catered halls of residence and apartments. Each apartment houses four to nine students in single rooms, each with its own toilet, sink, and shower and shared kitchen facilities. The university also puts up students in the University of London's nine intercollegiate halls, which offer a variety of different facilities for students of all colleges under the parent university's umbrella. King's student accommodation office supplies a list of roommate shares needed and wanted as well as a list of furnished flats for rent.

CAMPUS LIFE

There is no lack of activities either on or off campus for King's students. The college has its own student union, and students also have access to the University of London student union. One student reported that the union bars and nightclubs are actually fun (even though they are not considered to be "cool"). The college organizes freshers' activities at the beginning of the year and many events around Christmastime. But because King's is large, students say that it is not uncommon to fraternize only within their own academic schools and departments.

STUDENT 2 STUDENT

If you have any questions about academics or student life, why not ask a current student? King's runs a "student 2 student" telephone hot line for prospective students April 22 through July 11, 5:30–7:00 P.M. Call 44-207-848-4000 on the days designated for your study interests:

Mondays and Wednesdays—talk to students in the schools of Law, Humanities, Engineering, and Public Policy and Social Science.

Tuesdays and Thursdays—speak with students in the schools of Medicine, Dentistry, Nursing and Midwifery, Biomedical Science, and Health and Life Sciences.

ADMISSIONS AND FINANCIAL INFO

Students apply to King's College through UCAS (see page 245). Grants from the Overseas Hardship Fund may be available to American students who have already been accepted to the college but have come upon unexpected financial difficulties.

CONTACTS

King's College London
Strand, London
WC2R 2LS
England

Phone: 44-207-848-3051
E-mail: international@kcl.ac.uk
URL: www.kcl.ac.uk

London School of Economics and Political Science

London, England

AT A GLANCE

A prestigious university renowned for its achievements across a wide range of social, political, and economic sciences, the London School of Economics and Political Science (LSE) is part of the University of London system. It is known for its incredible diversity, both in its large international student body and in the range of its academics. One American college advisor compared it in scope to New York University.

Total Enrollment: 7,544; 2,909 U.K., 900 American
Undergraduate Enrollment: 3,602
Male/Female: 52/48
SAT Scores: Not required
Tuition: $15,990 per year

CAMPUS AND LOCATION

Since the school was founded in 1895, LSE has gained a reputation throughout the world for academic excellence. Thirteen Nobel Prize winners in economics, literature, and peace have been either LSE staff or alumni. There are many reasons to go to LSE, but students agree that the charm of the campus certainly is not one of them. Squished into already-cramped central London, the only place to go is up—additions are stacked on top of additions, creating a sort of tower of Babel. Most students don't mind what they say is an "utter lack of a campus," and enjoy the hustle and bustle of city life. For a frank, student-written guide to the school, visit **www.lse.ac.uk/collections/LSESU/alternativeProspectus**.

ACADEMICS

LSE offers 40 undergraduate degree programs across 18 academic departments and five interdisciplinary institutes. Although the LSE education is celebrated (and the degree is certainly prestigious), students are quick to point out that they are pretty much left on their own to sink or swim. Most professors are not especially accessible, and little importance is placed on assessing class work—students say that almost the entire grade rests on the final exam. Many students also report that first-year classes are not taken especially seriously, which can be good or bad, depending on your focus. If you're looking for more structure, or a shorter stay in London, you might want to consider the junior year abroad program called the General Course, during which visiting students are fully integrated into their university departments and are appointed a faculty member to be their personal tutor and to supervise them over the year.

FACILITIES

The British Library of Political and Economic Science is LSE's main library, and is the largest social sciences library in the world. Other learning facilities include the language center for classes and independent learning, over 30 research centers, and a newly built research lab. Students say that the extensive computer labs on campus make bringing your own computer a redundancy. Despite its central London location, LSE also has on-site badminton, squash, and gymnasium facilities, as well as its own 25-acre sports ground in Berrylands.

STUDENT HOUSING AND SERVICES

LSE currently has four halls of residence (Bankside House, Carr-Saunders Hall, Passfield Hall, and Rosebery Hall) and four self-catering blocks (Butlers Wharf, Great Dover Street, High Holborn, and 18 houses at Silver Walk in Rotherhithe). Together the residences accommodate more than 2,400 students and offer a variety of facilities (and costs). All overseas students are guaranteed accommodation in either an LSE or a University of London hall of residence. Students unanimously agree that the halls are great in terms of location and money—they are cheap and convenient. They are also great for socializing and making friends right away, but on the other hand, they can be very noisy with little room for personal space.

The student union provides financial aid, legal and welfare advice, health services, personal tutors, and support for students with disabilities. LSE Learning World offers classes and study skills advice.

CAMPUS LIFE

Although the student body at LSE is remarkably diverse, students say that at times this diversity can turn into cliquishness and separatism. As is the case with many urban colleges, students report that it is hard to meet people. Nonetheless, the student union organizes many clubs and activities and holds a freshers' fair for new students at the beginning of each school year. The athletic union, with over 2,000 members, organizes competitive and recreational sports teams and clubs like aerobics, men and women's basketball, rowing, extreme sports, and boxing. The student union also runs PuLSE, the school radio station, and *The Beaver*, the student newspaper, which is named after the school mascot. The LSE union features three cheap student bars, and some residences even have their own pubs. Otherwise, students venture out in the city of London to find virtually all forms of entertainment (underground, mainstream, and anything in between) at their fingertips.

ADMISSIONS AND FINANCIAL INFO

American high school qualifications are generally not enough to be considered for admission to LSE, but outstanding applicants who offer at least two (preferably three or four) AP tests with grades of 4 and 5 may be invited to take the LSE entrance exam. Held every March, the entrance exam is a three-hour test requiring no special preparation. It consists of essays on general discussion topics, a reading comprehension section, and math tests.

Applicants with one year of undergraduate study from a U.S. university require an overall GPA of 3.0 to 3.5. For specific course requirements, applicants should also refer to the individual degree program descriptions on LSE's web site. Students must apply through UCAS (see page 245).

CONTACTS

Student Recruitment Office
London School of Economics and Political Science
Houghton Street
London WC2A 2AE
England

Phone: 44-20-7955-6613
Fax: 44-20-7955-7421
E-mail: stu.rec@lse.ac.uk
URL: www.lse.ac.uk

Richmond, The American International University in London

London, England

AT A GLANCE

A small but very international American liberal arts university located across two campuses in London, Richmond is accredited in the U.S. and in the U.K., and graduates are awarded two degrees, one British and one American.

Undergraduate Enrollment: 1,000; 31% North American
(25% American), 15% Asian, 13% African, 13% Middle
Eastern, 12% European, 4% United Kingdom, 3% South
American
Male/Female: 75/25
Student/Faculty: 20/1
SAT Scores: 1050 required
Tuition: $16,650 per year
Accreditation: The Commission on Higher Education of the
Middle States Association of Colleges and Schools;
United Kingdom Open University Validation System

CAMPUS AND LOCATION

Richmond University was established in 1972 and occupies the Victorian buildings in Kensington that held the original Richmond College, which was once a part of the University of London. The Kensington campus is located in central London, in a fancy residential area known for its chichi department stores and beautiful parks. Another campus is located in South West London overlooking the river Thames and is about 30 minutes away from central London by the underground. This second campus, called the Richmond Hill campus, is home to most of the first- and second-year classes and lower-division dorms. Students feel that one of the more unfortunate aspects of life at Richmond is this segregation of upper- and lower-division students.

ACADEMICS

The Richmond education emphasizes multiculturalism. To this end, students are required to take certain courses outside of their major area of study that emphasize cultural exploration. These courses comprise the General Education Program. During their freshman year, all students must take the "common course," which is called Rights, Choices, and Values. Students must then choose five more introductory classes, one from each of the following areas: math, lab sciences, behavioral or social sciences, fine arts and theater, history, literature, or geography. Within these courses, students are encouraged to search for cultural comparisons and understandings. In their sophomore year, students choose an intermediate class from each of the following departments: Business; Computing, Math, and Science; Communication and Fine Arts; or Humanities and Social Science. During their freshman and sophomore years, students must also take at least three intercultural/international courses in total, and are also required to take two semesters of a foreign language or prove equivalent proficiency. In their junior and senior years, students must choose one course outside their major area of study from a list of upper-level multicultural courses.

Richmond offers a field studies program in which a small group of students and faculty spend a few weeks in another country studying the politics and culture. In the past, groups have gone to countries such as Morocco and China. Richmond also has two international study centers in Italy (one in Florence and one in Rome) that offer summer, semester, or yearlong courses in fine arts, culture, and language. The program in Florence also offers volunteer and internship programs in social sciences. Students who complete their sophomore year with a GPA of 2.5 or higher are eligible to participate in these programs. (See the school's web site at **www.richmond.ac.uk** for more details.)

FACILITIES

Each of Richmond's two campuses has its own library, and students at the Kensington campus also have access to the library at the nearby University of London Imperial College. Richmond University library staff can also help students obtain books from any of London's public or specialized libraries. Tech services and computer labs are also available at both campuses. Sports facilities available at the Richmond Hill campus include tennis, basketball, volleyball, and mini-soccer courts, and a weight/aerobics room. The Kensington campus doesn't have its own sports facilities, but students can use the well-equipped gym at Imperial College for a small fee. Other facilities on the Richmond Hill campus include a cafeteria, a campus store and mailroom, a coffee shop, and a student lounge with cable TV.

STUDENT HOUSING AND SERVICES

The main building at the Richmond Hill campus is an early nineteenth-century building which houses 170 students. Students have single or shared rooms with shared bathroom facilities. Students may also live in Montford House, located five minutes away from campus. These facilities are more like flats, and accommodate five people per apartment. At the Kensington campus, Atlantic House and Ambassador House accommodate 188 students and comprise the main residences. All rooms have private sinks and shared shower facilities. Atlantic House also accommodates the computer lab, cafeteria, campus store, mailroom, common room, and smoking lounge, making it the hub of student activity. The Metrogate Hotel is another student residence at the Kensington campus that offers 24-hour security, but it also imposes a midnight curfew on visitors. One former student who lived at this residence complained that the strict visitors' rules were "infantilizing." All students who live in university housing receive an 18-meal-per-week plan at the university cafeteria. Room and board costs are about $8,800 per year.

The department of student affairs at Richmond provides students with information on resident life, student activities, career development, counseling, and health education. An orientation is organized each year to walk new students through all aspects of university life and life in England. All students who are at Richmond for more than six months are entitled to use the British National Health Service. This medical plan usually does not cover dental care or specialized treatment.

CAMPUS LIFE

Extracurricular activities are an important part of life at Richmond, and student organizations are numerous. Some examples are the photo club, the Islamic society, the music club, the Pan-African society, the martial arts club, and the Mama Dance club, voted club of the year by the 2002 student body. Richmond also has a student literary publication and newspaper.

Social life off campus is as diverse as the city of London itself. A nearby chain pub called Finnegan's Wake is popular, as are small parties in the residence halls. Students have even devised creative solutions to get around the midnight guest curfew—when the night guards come by to check the rooms, guests are hidden in closets or on the roof. Residence halls have message boards for odd-job postings, and international students are often able to supplement their income by taking under-the-table dog-walking and baby-sitting jobs.

ADMISSIONS AND FINANCIAL INFO

Students generally need to have finished high school with a minimum GPA of 2.5 to be considered for admission. Students with advanced qualifications like A-Levels, the Baccalaureate, or AP test scores may be exempt from certain first-year courses. Contact the U.S. admissions office for scholarship details.

 CONTACTS

Richmond, The American International University in London
Queens Road
Richmond upon Thames
TW10 6JP
England

Continues ☞

Phone: 44-20-8332-9000
Fax: 44-20-8332-1596
E-mail: enroll@richmond.ac.uk
URL: www.richmond.ac.uk

U.S. Office of Admissions
Richmond, The American International University
   in London
343 Congress Street, Suite 3100
Boston, MA 02210

Phone: 617-450-5617
Fax: 617-450-5601
E-mail: us_admissions@richmond.ac.uk

Trinity College, University of Dublin

Dublin, Republic of Ireland

AT A GLANCE

Trinity College offers one of Ireland's most sought-after educations, and with 11% of its student body from outside the U.K., it is also one of the most diverse colleges in the country. It is widely celebrated for its prestige in the humanities and its traditional college atmosphere but not usually for its recreational or housing facilities.

Total Enrollment: 11,900; 88% Irish, 7% E.U., 3% North American, 2% other nationalities
Undergraduate Enrollment: 10,066
Male/Female: 40/60
SAT Scores: 1300 required
Tuition: $11,850–$15,527 per year, depending on the course

CAMPUS AND LOCATION

In 1592, Queen Elizabeth I founded Trinity College, based upon the college structure of Oxford and Cambridge. Trinity is Ireland's oldest university, and since its inception has been a leader in Ireland's research and teaching. The campus, which is spread out over 40 acres in Dublin, has come to define the city itself, with its grand cobblestone entranceway and many eighteenth-century buildings, most notably the Old Library. Despite its old look, Dublin is a young university town, with many trendy shops and ethnic restaurants, thrift stores, markets, and pubs and clubs galore. To check out what's going on this week in town, visit **www.eventguide.ie**.

Outside of the city, students enjoy exploring Ireland's green countryside and rolling hills. Mountain walks, castles, and beaches are less than an hour's drive away, and Dublin's coastal location even allows you to take a ferry to France, Spain, or England for the day.

ACADEMICS

Trinity offers undergraduate degrees across its six faculties: Arts (Humanities); Arts (Letters); Business, Economic and Social Studies; Engineering and Systems Sciences; Health Sciences; and Science. The education is somewhat broad in that it allows students to take courses from within different faculties. The school year is divided into three terms: Michaelmas (nine weeks, October–December);

Hilary (nine weeks, January–March); and Trinity (six weeks, April–May), with a four-week exam period at the end of the year. At the beginning of their academic careers, each student is assigned a tutor in their area of study to advise them and offer some supervision for the remainder of their degree program.

FACILITIES

Old Library, Trinity College's main library, is one of the largest in Europe. Since 1801 the library has received all materials copyrighted in Ireland and the U.K., and it now has over four million books as well as an extensive collection of manuscripts, maps, and music. Other facilities include the Trinity College Enterprise Center, the Arts and Social Science Building, College Park (where the sports fields are located), dining halls, cafeterias, and bars. There is no formal student center, and students complain that the sports facilities are subpar.

STUDENT HOUSING AND SERVICES

Since the college is in an urban setting, most students find it just as convenient to live in their own apartments in Dublin or in arranged homestays. Less than ten percent of students live on campus. For those who do want university accommodations, Trinity provides a limited number of college rooms in shared houses or small self-catered flats in the inner suburbs of the city. Most cost between $300 and $400 per month. The College does not have a meal plan, but the catering department has some food outlets around campus, and the college's main dining hall serves both lunch and Commons, the traditional formal evening meal.

Trinity's health center is especially comprehensive and offers students a number of primary care services and clinics covering mental health, birth control, sports medicine, and a number of other issues. The college also provides career and academic advising and a chaplaincy. An orientation is arranged for all new and international students during Freshers' Week at the beginning of every fall term.

CAMPUS LIFE

Life at Trinity is reported to be chock-full of things to do, both on and off campus. The Central Societies Committee is the body responsible for the almost 100 student societies at Trinity, including one of Ireland's oldest debate teams. Organized sports clubs (both recreational and competitive) include traditional sports as well as windsurfing, ultimate Frisbee, and trampolining. Trinity is right in the center of town, so when the two campus bars close at 11, students can take advantage of Dublin's vibrant cultural scene and nightlife. The Temple Bar area across from the main gates of campus is popular for its many pubs and restaurants, but experienced students recommend exploring some of the less touristy parts of town.

ADMISSIONS AND FINANCIAL INFO

American students should apply to the office of International Student Affairs. Entry qualifications vary depending on course, but in general, admissions are selective. Trinity offers no financial aid for entering American students, but in their second year students can take a scholarship exam to be eligible for up to one third off tuition fees.

 CONTACTS

**The Office of International Student Affairs,
Trinity College**
Dublin 2
Ireland

Phone: 35-31-608-2011
Fax: 35-31-677-1698
E-mail: ISA.Office@tcd.ie
URL: www.tcd.ie

University of Cambridge

Cambridge, England

AT A GLANCE

The University of Cambridge is one of the most prestigious univer-sities in the world and one of the largest in the U.K. Based on a sys-tem similar to that of the University of Oxford (see page 297), Cambridge is made up of many semiautonomous colleges that offer personalized teaching. For its strengths across all academic areas, the *Times Good Universities Guide,* a prominent annual U.K. pub-lication, has listed Cambridge at the top of its rankings every year. The quality of a Cambridge education is certainly not in question, but from what we've heard, the learning environment can be a bit stuffy. One student mentioned to us that some of the university's routines seemed to be as old as the school itself.

Total Enrollment: 16,500; 3.1% E.U., 7.3% other
  nationalities
Undergraduate Enrollment: 11,600
Male/Female: 55/45
Tuition: $11,617–$15,213 per year

CAMPUS AND LOCATION

The University of Cambridge's first colleges were founded in 1284, making it one of the oldest universities in the world. Today its 31 colleges sprawl across the town of Cambridge, a picturesque cobblestone hamlet that dates back to medieval times. Close your eyes and picture a bespectacled undergrad in a tweed blazer riding by on a bike, books piled on the back fender, college scarf flying in the wind. Imagine a town full of such academics, sharing stories in college pubs, stopping to chat with their professors in the archways of gothic buildings, relaxing under trees on perfectly manicured lawns. That's Cambridge for you. The cozy college town is characterized by the presence of the university (and sometimes by tourists, who flock to check out Cambridge's legendary traditional charm). It's got pubs and clubs, a thriving music scene, movie theaters, cafés and restaurants, and decent shopping, but if you're looking for more, hop on a train and head to London, which is less than an hour away.

ACADEMICS

Cambridge University is divided into two levels: the colleges and the university. The university awards degrees, but each college is responsible for hiring its own professors and admitting its own students. Classes are taught through departments at both the college and the university level.

Degree courses (called Triposes) are divided into two parts spanning three years. In some subjects there is a two-year Part I (which may be divided into Part IA and Part IB) and a one-year Part II. In others, Part I lasts for one year, Part II for two years. In engineering and some science subjects there is a fourth year (Part II or III) leading to a more specialized degree. At the end of each Part, students must pass exams to move on to the next level. Most students take successive Parts of the same Tripos, but it is possible to switch Tripos (usually within a related field) after Part I or Part IA. This makes for a wide array of degree options.

One of the main benefits of a Cambridge education is the supervision system, which allows students to gain an intense level of specialization in a subject. Similar to tutorials at Oxford, supervisions are meetings with a senior member of a faculty, department or college for individuals, pairs, or small groups of students. Supervisions are supplemented by broader lectures or discussion-based classes and seminars in which dissertations and research projects play a significant role.

Cambridge has study abroad exchange programs with universities around the world. For example, through the Cambridge-MIT Institute, students from Cambridge can study at MIT for a year. In general, though, students are not admitted to Cambridge on a part-time or visiting-student basis. A friend of ours who wanted to go to Cambridge for her junior year actually had to transfer out of her college, apply to Cambridge as a first-year, and then transfer the credits back to her university after a year. It was complicated, but she found it to be totally worthwhile.

FACILITIES

Cambridge gives students access to an excellent range of research facilities. Each college has its own library, each department or faculty library has a collection of more specialized materials, and, as a last resort, the university library (commonly referred to as the UL) has a copy of nearly every book published in the U.K., as well as a large international collection. The university language center is impressive, with materials available in over 120 languages. The university, departments, and colleges all provide computer labs. The university also has eight specialist museums and collections as well as a botanical garden and Kettle's Yard (a concert hall). Sports and recreational facilities are found university-wide at each college.

STUDENT HOUSING AND SERVICES

Almost all undergraduate students live in college accommodations. Facilities vary throughout the colleges—some are modern dorm complexes, some are more old-fashioned, but most are singles with internet connections and catering facilities. Students enjoy the convenience and community feeling of living in the same place that their supervisions are held and where they can socialize in the college pub. Each college has its own history and traditions, and some even require students to wear their gowns (as in cap and gown, not ball gown) to dinner in the dining hall.

A variety of services are offered to help international students integrate into the rest of the student body. Health, career, and personal and academic counseling are available, and CUSU International, an autonomous part of the Cambridge University student union, is dedicated to representing the needs of overseas students on campus.

CAMPUS LIFE

There are a number of university-sponsored societies, including the renowned Amateur Dramatics Club, which spawned the careers of Michael Palin and Emma Thompson, among other actors. The university also sponsors a number of well-attended events throughout the year, such as the Societies Fair each October and an elaborate black-tie spring ball featuring carnival rides. Most colleges have their own clubs and societies, offering a variety of nonacademic activities. For the student union's web site, featuring a guide to Cambridge and the many student events around the city, visit **www.cusu.cam.ac.uk**.

ADMISSIONS AND FINANCIAL INFO

One would imagine that a university as prestigious as Cambridge would be very difficult to get into . . . and it is! (In 2002, the university had only a 30% acceptance rate.) Students coming from American high schools should get in touch with the individual colleges or the admissions office as early as possible to discuss their qualifications. Students must apply through UCAS by October 15, and also through the Cambridge admissions form. The form should be sent either to your chosen college or to the Cambridge admissions office if you are making an open application (i.e., letting the university decide which college to put you in). For information on specific colleges, visit the web site at **www.cam.ac.uk/cambuniv/ugprospectus**.

Overseas applicants may be considered without an interview and can sometimes be interviewed in their own countries.

CONTACTS

Cambridge Admissions Office
Kellet Lodge
Tennis Court Road
Cambridge CB2 1QJ
England

Phone: 44-12-2333-3308
Fax: 44-12-2336-6383
E-mail: undergrad-enquiries@cuao.cam.ac.uk
URL: www.cam.ac.uk (This web site also has contact
    information for the individual colleges.)

University College London

London, England

AT A GLANCE

University College London was founded in 1826 as the first college of the University of London (which has since expanded to include over 20 autonomous colleges and institutes). It boasts many famous alumni, including Robert Browning, Mahatma Gandhi, Justine Frischmann (front woman for the band Elastica), three members of Coldplay, and 18 Nobel Prize winners.

Total Enrollment: 15,713; 5.5% E.U., 14% international
Undergraduate Enrollment: 10,337
Student/Faculty: 6/1
SAT Scores: 1300 required
Tuition: $15,000 per year
Affiliation: European Consortium of International Schools
(ECIS) Member

CAMPUS AND LOCATION

The main campus of University College is located near Euston Station in Bloomsbury, an area famous for its intellectual history (home to Virginia Woolf's legendary Bloomsbury Group), museums, parks, and great restaurants.

ACADEMICS

University College offers three types of undergraduate degrees in over 200 program areas—single-subject honors degrees, which are like a regular B.A. or B.S. degree; combined studies honors degrees, in which two subject areas are studied; and cross-disciplinary degrees, where students build a degree from a range of disciplines. Degrees normally take three years to complete and are organized on a course unit system. Each program is structured differently, but in general students must take about four course units per year. (Some degree programs do not follow this system, so check with the individual departments for more information.) Students usually spend about 15 hours a week in lectures, seminars, and tutorials. (For science and engineering students, it's about 20.) Each student is assigned to a tutor or academic advisor. Assessment is based on assignments throughout the year and final exams. Students must pass at least three exams to go on to their next level.

University College offers study abroad exchanges with over 170 universities worldwide.

FACILITIES

UCL's main library has many specialist branches and special teaching and research collections, including the Petrie Museum of Egyptian Archaeology, the College Art Collection, the Grant Museum of Zoology, and the Geological Sciences Collection. There are about 1,000 PCs on campus in computer labs and in residences. The language center offers a variety of foreign language courses as well as the Self-Access Center for individual language learning. Sports facilities are provided in the Bloomsbury Fitness Center and the Somers Town Sports Center. UCL also has a huge professional-quality sports ground at Shenley, Hertfordshire.

STUDENT HOUSING AND SERVICES

All first-years are guaranteed housing placement if they apply on time and have not previously been a degree student in London. University College offers two halls of residence, Ifor Evans Hall in Camden Town and Ramsey Hall in Bloomsbury. Both have small kitchens on each floor, laundry facilities, TV lounges, game rooms, a computer lab, and a pub. There are many other smaller student houses. All are self-catered with large shared kitchens in the basement. Students report that the halls are comfortable, very convenient to major tube lines, and located in a safe part of Bloomsbury. Their only real drawback is the lack of closet space. Students may also apply to live in the University of London's intercollegiate halls.

UCL offers a full range of health services, including a dental practice and physician house calls. Confidential personal counseling is also available, and at the beginning of the year students are assigned a personal tutor to help them through academic issues. The UCL Student Union Rights and Advice Center gives students financial and personal assistance, and there are also special women students advisors and an international office.

CAMPUS LIFE

The UCL student union organizes some 150-plus student societies and many events and parties at its numerous student bars. For an e-mail directory to student clubs and for events listings, visit **www.uclu.org.**

The college has its very own West End theater, where at least ten weeks each year are dedicated to student productions put on through the dance, music, and drama societies. The sports union organizes clubs for many sports, including football, rowing, women's rugby, kung fu, water polo, and skateboarding.

Find out about student life firsthand through the "ask a student" page on the UCL web site. To e-mail your questions to current students, go to **www.ucl.ac.uk/prospective-students/widening-participation.**

ADMISSIONS AND FINANCIAL INFO

Students applying directly from an American high school must have a score of at least 4 in four AP tests. Otherwise, students must have completed one year at a recognized U.S. university. Apply through UCAS by January 15 for fall entry. (For more info on UCAS, see page 245.)

A number of £3,000 scholarships are available to U.S. students. For more information, contact the Entrance Scholarships Office at 44-20-7679-7385 or **scholarships@ucl.ac.uk.**

CONTACTS

The International Office
University College London
Gower Street
London WC1E 6BT
England

Phone: 44-20-7679-7765
Fax: 44-20-7679-3001
E-mail: international@ucl.ac.uk
URL: www.ucl.ac.uk

University of Edinburgh

Edinburgh, Scotland

AT A GLANCE

The University of Edinburgh was founded in 1583, and in the past 400 years has built a strong reputation in the arts, medicine, and sciences. Walter Scott, Charles Darwin, and Robert Louis Stevenson are just a few of its famous alumni. It also offers a freshman-year study abroad program, which allows American students to ease their way into the Scottish educational system.

Total Enrollment: 21,000; 4,000 international
Undergraduate Enrollment: 16,000
Male/Female: 50/50
Student/Faculty: 12/1
SAT Scores: 1200 required
Tuition: $12,000 per year

CAMPUS AND LOCATION

The University of Edinburgh is broken up into five campuses across the city. The main campus is near George Square, close to the center of town and to the historic Royal Mile. Other campuses include the Holyrood campus for education and the King's Buildings campus for science and engineering. As first impressions go, Edinburgh (population 500,000) makes a very dramatic one. It is situated on a hill running down to the sea, and neoclassical columns and a twelfth-century castle tower over the compact city. The city hosts a number of annual international events such as the Edinburgh International Arts Festival, the Fringe Festival, a film festival, and a book festival. Each holiday season, Edinburgh transforms into a winter wonderland for its Christmas Festival (complete with outdoor ice-skating and Christmas markets) that culminates in Hogmanay, a four-day party bonanza.

Edinburgh is also cosmopolitan, with a vibrant club, music, and film scene for its many student inhabitants to enjoy. Although the city is small enough to be easily walkable, an efficient public bus system makes it even easier to get around. Another reason students love Edinburgh is its liberal licensing policy, which means that pubs stay open past midnight (something that is pretty rare in the U.K.). For students who feel like stretching their legs, the picturesque Scottish Highlands, coastline, and hills are only a few hours away by train or car.

ACADEMICS

The University of Edinburgh offers over 300 degrees across three colleges: the College of Social Sciences, the College of Medicine and Veterinary Medicine, and the College of Science and Engineering. Degree programs can be relatively broad; during their first year, students normally take courses in three or more subjects and then narrow the subjects down to two or three in the second year. Also, students don't need to decide on their degree program until the end of their second year. Courses are usually taught through a combination of lectures (sometimes as large as 150 in the first-year classes), group tutorials, and seminars and through labs and hands-on classes for science-based subjects. The university also offers a freshman year abroad program. In this program, American students start off their first year with a less specialized curriculum so that at the end of the year they can more easily transfer to another university or decide to join the rest of the student body.

FACILITIES

The Main Library, located in George Square, was founded in 1580 and is one of the largest academic libraries in the world. The university's computer services is the largest in the U.K., with computer labs across all campuses, even some 24-hour ones. The university's art is housed in the Talbot Rice Gallery, comprised of the Red Gallery, a classics collection, and the White Gallery, a modern collection.

The University of Edinburgh's sports center boasts a large gym, a swimming pool, eight glass-backed squash courts, two hard-backed squash courts, two weight-training gyms, a free-weights room, a circuit-training gym, a combat salle, a rifle range, an archery range, a boxing gym, three multipurpose rooms, and a top-class fitness assessment and sports injuries clinic. The Firbush Point Field Center is an outdoor sports center located on the south shore of Loch Tay in Perthshire (80 miles from Edinburgh). Firbush provides activities and courses in sailing, canoeing, skiing, and mountaineering.

A view of the ancient city of Edinburgh shows the
University of Edinburgh's spires in the distance.

STUDENT HOUSING AND SERVICES

The University of Edinburgh houses approximately 5,600 students
in three types of accommodation—halls of residence, self-catering
residences, and university flats—all in central Edinburgh within a
mile of the main campus. All rooms have central heating, almost all
are singles, and about a quarter of them offer private bathrooms.
All first-year students are guaranteed university accommodations.

Student support is offered through career counseling, a chaplaincy, health services with a pharmacy, a learning and resource
center, and The Advice Place, a drop-in advice center run by professional staff and student volunteers. International students are eligible for free National Health Service treatment.

CAMPUS LIFE

Extracurricular life at the university revolves around the Edinburgh
Union Student Association (EUSA). The EUSA buildings, located

across all campuses, provide a good (and cheap) venue for drinking, dancing, and checking out live music and DJs and the rest of EUSA's varied entertainment programs. EUSA also funds about 170 student societies covering a huge array of interests, "no matter how bizarre." It organizes Rag Week, a charity event with fundraising festivities such as film festivals and tequila drinking and bartending contests. For more information on student life, visit **www.eusa.ed.ac.uk.**

ADMISSIONS AND FINANCIAL INFO

Requirements vary across the colleges; students are advised to contact the international office before applying. Students applying to the freshman year abroad program should submit applications through the international office. All other students should apply directly through UCAS. (See page 245 for more information.)

 CONTACTS

Alan Mackay, International Officer
The International Office
The University of Edinburgh
57 George Square
Edinburgh EH8 9JU
Scotland

Phone: 44-13-1650-4198
Fax: 44-13-1668-4565
E-mail: a.mackay@ed.ac.uk
URL: www.ed.ac.uk

University of Kent at Canterbury

Canterbury, England

AT A GLANCE

The University of Kent is a medium-sized modern university in a picturesque and small, but lively, college town. One U.S. college counselor highly recommended Kent as a real "college-y" college, offering students a sense of community and campus culture that is lacking at many U.K. universities.

> **Total Enrollment:** 7,294; 23% international
> **Undergraduate Enrollment:** 6,348
> **Male/Female:** 45/55
> **Student/Faculty:** 18/1
> **Tuition:** $11,696–$15,220 per year, depending on course

CAMPUS AND LOCATION

The University of Kent was founded in 1965 as part of England's "new universities" movement in the '60s. Although that term is now obsolete, the university still maintains a "modern" image, with its contemporary architecture and emphasis on interdisciplinary studies in the humanities and social sciences. (The university also boasts of its "groundbreaking" achievements in technology and medical sciences.)

Kent's modern buildings are situated on 300 acres landscaped with gardens, ponds, and woods, about a 20-minute walk from the center of Canterbury. Canterbury is a small and friendly college town that has been inhabited since pre-Roman times. Augustine established its first cathedral in 600 A.D. This famous cathedral is also the venue for the University of Kent's degree ceremonies. In medieval times the city was a center for pilgrimage to the shrine of St. Thomas à Becket, and the stories of these pilgrims inspired Chaucer's *Canterbury Tales*. Canterbury is about 50 miles away from London.

ACADEMICS

Kent has 18 academic departments that are divided into three faculties—Humanities and Social Sciences, Science and Technology, and Medical Studies. The university offers single, joint, and multidisciplinary honors degree programs, as well as four-year programs that combine language courses and study abroad experience. Many applied sciences programs also offer four-year degree programs with an initial foundation year for students without the qualifications to enter into the regular three-year program. A unique aspect of academics at Kent is its "Level 1" program, taken in the first academic year. It is necessary to pass Level 1 to move on to the second year, but results do not count toward the class of your degree because of the interdisciplinary nature of the Level 1 program. At the end of the first year, students have the option to continue in their current degree programs or change subjects.

FACILITIES

Kent offers some great arts facilities, like the Gulbenkian Theater, a 340-seat capacity venue with a lobby café/bar for university departments, as well as for touring theater companies and professional musicians. Cinema 3 is Kent's own art-house movie theater, open to the general public. It has ties to the film studies program and is involved in Canterbury's annual international film festival. The campus sports center features a climbing wall, a gym, a solarium and sauna, a sports injury clinic, a sports shop, outdoor tennis courts and playing fields, a new sports pavilion, and a flood-lit all-weather field for soccer and hockey. Each college also has its own academic and recreational facilities.

STUDENT HOUSING AND SERVICES

There are two general types of accommodations offered on campus, standard and superior—superior being the more popular and expensive of the two options. Within these categories, accommodations vary throughout the colleges but rooms are mainly singles on coed halls. Smoking and nonsmoking floors are available, as are rooms with internet connections (for an extra charge).

Student learning advisory services runs workshops on academic issues, and the student union advice and information services help students with financial, immigration, and legal problems. The chaplaincy leads multifaith services. A general practitioner serves students at the on-campus medical center, and a disabilities support center helps students with physical and learning problems.

CAMPUS LIFE

Student life revolves around Kent's four residential colleges, each named after a distinguished British figure—Darwin, Keynes (economist), Eliot (poet), and Rutherford (physicist). Kent likes to think of each college as a "ready-made community." All students and staff are members of a specific college, even if they live off campus. Each college has a college master responsible for the welfare of their students and also a junior college committee that organizes student activities.

The student union also provides many services and recreational facilities. The 1,200-capacity student union "Venue" was opened in 1998 and houses three bars that are open until 2 A.M. six nights a week, as well as The Lighthouse, a Mediterranean bistro. Recent visiting acts include Kula Shaker and the Divine Comedy (two great British bands that never quite made it in the United States). Woody's bar is another campus pub that serves food and has a big-screen satellite TV. The bars on campus host many live music events and guest DJs. (For more information about the student union, visit **www.kentunion.co.uk.**)

Kent also sponsors many student societies (such as *Star Trek,* wine tasting, and ballroom dancing societies), a student newspaper, and the oldest student-run radio station in the country. Although there is no degree in music at the university, the student union and Kent's own director of music organize many extracurricular music programs. There is a chorus, a symphony orchestra, and a concert band that are open to all interested musicians, and an auditioned chamber choir. The Gulbenkian Theater hosts many concerts, and each year students work alongside professionals to put on Kent's annual summer opera.

ADMISSIONS AND FINANCIAL INFO

Apply through UCAS (see page 245). Students with American high school qualifications may also need AP test scores. A limited number of merit-based scholarships may be available to international students. Contact the international office for more details.

CONTACTS

International Office
The Registry
University of Kent at Canterbury
Canterbury, Kent CT2 7NZ
England

Phone: 44-12-2782-3905
Fax: 44-12-2782-3247
E-mail: International-office@ukc.ac.uk
URL: www.ukc.ac.uk

University of Oxford

Oxford, England

AT A GLANCE

Founded in 1167, Oxford is the oldest English-language university in the world—and one of the most selective. Located in the archetypal college town, it is broken up into many smaller colleges, each with their own traditions and impressive cast of alumni: Sir Thomas More, Sir Walter Raleigh, Thomas Hobbes and Jonathan Locke, Sir Christopher Wren, Oscar Wilde, Margaret Thatcher, Tony Blair, Bill Clinton, and Theodore "Dr. Seuss" Geisel to name a few.

Total Enrollment: 16,500
Undergraduate Enrollment: 11,500
Male/Female: 58/42
SAT Scores: 1400 required
Tuition: $13,000–$17,000 per year, not including a
$6,400 annual college fee

CAMPUS AND LOCATION

Oxford University's centuries-long tradition of achievement has historically been based in the humanities, but since the 1930s the university has come into its own in applied science research facilities.

The university and its 39 separate colleges dominate all aspects of life in the town of Oxford. It is a beautiful, charming medieval town with soaring cathedral spires and old stone buildings. It also has all of the conveniences of a modern city, and a hip one at that. Its 30,000-some-odd student population enjoys a large selection of shopping, clubs, pubs and bars, art galleries, theaters, cinemas, and international restaurants. Oxford also has a great music scene. Check out **www.oxfordbands.com** for info on local music, and **www.cheeky-chops.freeserve.co.uk/cheeky/oxford/thebook.html** for a humorous, slightly subversive guide to the city. The town sponsors a number of yearly events such as the St. Giles' Fair and Carnival. On May Day at dawn a choir sings a call to summer from the top of the Magdalen College Tower, and the event, which draws big crowds, is often followed by partying into the wee hours. In June the town comes together again for Summer Eights, the university's annual rowing competition among its colleges. If Oxford just doesn't cut it for you, London is about a three-hour drive away.

ACADEMICS

The university is divided into 39 colleges. All undergraduates are members of a college. The colleges act as the hub of a student's social and academic life at Oxford, and each has its own distinct personality. The individual colleges are responsible for selecting their own undergraduate students, providing residence, academic, and recreational facilities, as well as pastoral services. The university organizes lectures and seminars, provides many academic resources, and is responsible for organizing exams and giving out grades.

The teaching method at Oxford combines lectures and some seminars with private tutorials. Students take tutorials in their specializations, meeting with their tutors one-on-one once or twice a week to discuss and go over work and research students have prepared on their own. Students are assigned tutors at their own colleges, but if their subject area requires more in-depth analysis, tutors can recommend that students have tutorials at other colleges as well. Tutors also help students organize university lectures and courses to fit into their curriculum. Most courses follow the same syllabus throughout the colleges because lectures and exams are organized at the university level. Oxford students enjoy the best of both worlds—the learning tools of a very large university combined with the individual attention of a very small college.

Students must be extremely self-reliant and motivated to succeed at Oxford. This phenomenon can be seen in the university's exam policy. The university usually gives only two sets of exams throughout the degree program—at the beginning of the course in the first year, to see if the student can continue with the course, and at the end of the course in the third year, usually through a series of papers. All Oxford degree programs have their own core elements as well as electives.

FACILITIES

Since students are essentially responsible for creating the content of their tutorials, the university strives to provide them with some of the best learning and research facilities in the world. Each college has its own library, and the university itself has a number of libraries. The Bodleian Library is the main research library of the university and has a number of branches, like the Old Library, New Library, Radcliffe Camera, and other specialized branches. The Bodleian Library is as beautiful as it is functional, and it attracts many tourists and hosts classical music concerts. There are many other special collections throughout the university, and many faculties have their own collections. (For more info on Oxford's libraries, visit **www.lib.ox.ac.uk.**)

Oxford University computer services provides technical support and network access to all university students as well as computer training programs and a discounted computer store. The university language center is open to all students for credit and extracurricular language study and research. Oxford University also has a number of renowned museums and art galleries—the Asmolean Museum of Art and Archaeology, the University Museum of Natural History, the Pitt Rivers Museum of Ethnography, and the Museum of the History of Science. (Visit **www.ox.ac.uk/ museums** for more information.) There is also a beautiful botanical garden. Each college has its own dining rooms, pubs, and recreational and sports facilities. The university itself has a large athletics center and sports field.

STUDENT HOUSING AND SERVICES

Students are housed in their residential colleges, so facilities vary significantly. All on-campus rooms are equipped with a sink, desk, bed, and lamps. Some dorms have kitchens and some are catered. Housing costs also vary significantly from college to college.

Each college is responsible for the welfare of its students and provides its own personal and academic counseling services. The colleges also have their own nurses on duty during the week for minor emergencies, as well as NHS (National Health Services) doctors. The university itself offers counseling outside the colleges with the University Counseling Service, staffed by professional counselors and therapists, and the Oxford Nightline, a hot line run by students from 8 P.M. to 8 A.M. every night. Careers services helps students find part-time and volunteer work and has a reputation for getting students jobs after graduation.

CAMPUS LIFE

Each college has what is known as a Junior Common Room, or JCR. This name refers to the elected committee that represents its undergraduate student body. These students act as a sort of mini student union and plan events for the colleges. All Oxford students have access to Oxford University's student union. The Oxford student union provides student services like legal and welfare advice, organizes university-wide events like the Freshers' Fair, and plans intercollegiate activities.

ADMISSIONS AND FINANCIAL INFO

Oxford is a very tough school to get into, especially for candidates coming directly from American high schools. The university itself has no formal entry qualifications, but Oxford strongly advises students to contact the tutor for admissions at their college of preference for more information. Apply through UCAS by October 15, and keep in mind that you cannot apply to both Oxford and Cambridge in the same year. (For more information on UCAS, see page 245.)

About 85% of students apply directly to a specific college, but if you're unsure about which college is right for you, submit what is known as an open application. In this case, the university matches students to a college based on their qualifications and interests. Students should keep in mind that it is usually impossible to switch colleges after being admitted, so it is recommended that you do some research before applying. For information on specific colleges, visit **www.admissions.ox.ac.uk/colleges**. If you do decide to make an open application, contact Dr. Barbara Kennedy, the university's international recruitment officer, at **irc@admin.ox.ac.uk**.

As interviews are usually a fundamental part of the application process, Oxford sends faculty to North America, usually to Vancouver and New York, every fall to interview candidates. Oxford does not accept transfer applications; students who wish to leave their present university to come to Oxford have to start over from square one.

 CONTACTS

International Recruitment Officer/Oxford Colleges Admissions Office/University Offices
Wellington Square
Oxford OX1 2JD
England

Phone: 44-18-6528-8000
E-mail: irc@admin.ox.ac.uk,
    undergraduate.admissions@admin.ox.ac.uk
URL: www.ox.ac.uk

University of St. Andrews

St. Andrews, Scotland

AT A GLANCE

St. Andrews was voted the University of the Year in 2002 by the U.K.'s *Sunday Times University Guide* and is one of the top universities in the U.K. (good enough even for Prince William). St. Andrews is also one of the most popular destinations for Americans looking to leave the States for college, due in part to the university's recruitment efforts and also because of its academic structure, which is somewhat more flexible than most universities in the U.K.

> **Total Enrollment:** 6,000; 22% international
> **Undergraduate Enrollment:** 5,500
> **Male/Female:** 48/52
> **SAT Scores:** 1250 required
> **Tuition:** $12,974–$15,491 per year

CAMPUS AND LOCATION

Founded in 1411, St. Andrews is Scotland's first university. The sprawling Gothic campus is located in picturesque St. Andrews, a quaint college town with a population of 16,000. The town offers many cultural attractions, pubs, a beach, and a world-famous cashmere outlet. It also just happens to be the birthplace of golf. (Its "Old Course," which is the world's first golf course, draws many visitors year-round.) Students generally rave about the small and traditional town by the sea. One student told us that she loves walking around town and running into students and professors, but that sometimes, "it's like living in a little bubble." Probably the worst thing about life in St. Andrews is the weather—"cold, rainy, and windy almost the whole year round."

ACADEMICS

Academics at St. Andrews are flexible and require a lot of independence. We've heard that the "level of academic difficulty is really up to the student—you get back what you put in. No one is going to chase you." Some students feel that they are left too much on their own. "You are expected to solve your own academic problems—there is little help from the tutors."

The university offers many degrees across its three faculties of Arts, Science, and Divinity. English, Economics, and International Relations are reported to be especially strenuous areas of study.

St. Andrews' four-year undergraduate degree programs have a special component specifically for its American student body. Their first year, American students follow a general curriculum designed so that at the end of the year they can either transfer back to the States or join the rest of the student body. Those students who remain spend the second year taking modules in three to five different subject areas, and then, in the final two years, specialize in one or more subjects. This is quite a change from the rigid nature of most universities in the U.K., and most students really appreciate that they can put off having to decide what type of degree to take until the end of their second year.

FACILITIES

Some students feel that facilities at St. Andrews are a bit skimpy. The library is small but adequate, and the computer labs cannot always support the volume of students. (Students recall how in recent memory the St. Andrews network crashed and caused total chaos, especially since there aren't any internet cafés in town.) The sports center consists solely of a weight room and some playing fields, so many students join the leisure center in town in order to use the pool.

STUDENT HOUSING AND SERVICES

The university provides housing for two-thirds of its students, giving priority to first-years. Accommodations vary from traditional catered residence halls to self-catered flats. Students advise trying to get a spot in one of the bigger residence halls in town, which are nicer, cleaner, and more fun (i.e., closer to the older students and pubs).

In the way of student support, St. Andrews offers a health center, psychological and academic counseling, and a chaplaincy. The Overseas Society, the student union, and the student services office provide additional support.

CAMPUS LIFE

Students reportedly party as much as they study, no small task at such an academically competitive university. One student told us, "Go to St. Andrews for a good time, but don't expect radical politics or too much diversity." Another student made reference to the lack of political involvement in the student body, calling it "St. Andrews apathy."

Whether they like each other or not, though, students do tend to spend a lot of time together. Over half of St. Andrews' students live on campus, so as in the most fun American universities, there's a blurry line between academics and social life. One student said that St. Andrews was "not really a 'campus,' but more like a friendly town." The student union sponsors nearly 100 recreational clubs, over 50 sports clubs, a radio station, and student publications. The music center provides practice facilities and extracurricular classes to over 500 students. Each year the union holds an event called "Give It a Go" for new students to check out its many activities.

The student union building offers little in the way of recreation (it's pretty much just a game room and a pub with some pool ta-

St. Salvator's Quad at the
University of St. Andrews in Scotland

bles, mainly frequented by first-years), except when it shows sports events on its big-screen TV. To really let their hair down, though, students head into town to visit the many pubs and bars. Some of the most popular ones are the Westport, a minimalist and trendy bar; the Vic, which is known for its karaoke nights; the Raisin; and MaBelles, known for attracting a large proportion of "rugby boys." Some students complained that there is a serious "lack of alternative things to do in town apart from drinking," and also that there aren't any clubs for dancing. Wednesday nights, the student union hires a bus so that students can go clubbing in Dundee, a town about a half hour away. Students also report that "every weekend there are usually a bunch of house parties, which are fun."

ADMISSIONS AND FINANCIAL INFO

Candidates from North America who aren't applying to any other universities in the U.K. may apply using the Direct Enrollment Application Form on the university web site. Otherwise, North American students must apply through UCAS (see page 245).

 CONTACTS

The International Office
University of St. Andrews
Butts Wynd
St. Andrews, Fife
Scotland
KY16 9AJ

Phone: 44-13-3446-3323
Fax: 44-13-3446-3330
E-mail: intoff@st-and.ac.uk
URL: www.st-andrews.ac.uk

University of Stirling

Stirling, Scotland

AT A GLANCE

With strong academics (*The Sunday Times University Guide* ranked it sixteenth in the U.K. for teaching quality in 2001), and one of the most beautiful campuses in the U.K., this modern Scottish university is well worth looking into. Students come to Stirling for its flexible academics (you can change your major up to the second year) and its "welcoming atmosphere."

> **Total Enrollment:** 9,000
> **Undergraduate Enrollment:** 7,000; 2,000 international
> **SAT Scores:** 1100 required
> **Tuition:** $9,959–$13,146 per year

CAMPUS AND LOCATION

The University of Stirling's main Parkland campus was built in 1967 on the 300-acre estate of eighteenth-century Airthrey Castle. Its mostly modern buildings, centered on a large loch, seem to disappear into the campus's lush landscaping and breathtaking views of the surrounding Ochil Hills. (Stirling also has two smaller campuses for nursing and midwifery students: the Highlands campus in Inverness and the Western Isles campus in Stornoway.) The Parkland campus lies just on the outskirts of Stirling, one of Scotland's oldest towns with a population of about 40,000 (20% of which are students). Its quaint and historic Victorian city center offers such attractions as a movie theater, a bowling alley, an ice rink, and a water park. When the cozy town gets claustrophobic, students head for Glasgow or Edinburgh, about 45 minutes away by car. For more on Stirling, visit **www.stirling.co.uk**.

ACADEMICS

Stirling prides itself on the flexible nature of its degree programs. Undergraduate courses are offered in the Faculty of Arts, Faculty of Human Sciences, Faculty of Management, and Faculty of Natural Sciences, but students can often take classes across more than one faculty. Courses are taught through a pretty standard lecture, seminar, and tutorial arrangement, but many classes also emphasize fieldwork. Students take three courses a semester, which are assessed throughout the year and also during an exam period.

FACILITIES

The modern Stirling Library and 24-hour computer labs contrast architecturally with the refurbished eighteenth-century Aithery Castle, which houses the Center for English Language Teaching and the Division of Academic Innovation and Continuing Education. Athletic facilities include the Gannochy Sports Center, home to the National Swimming Academy and the Scottish National Tennis Center, as well as a nine-hole golf course and driving range. Students can also use the Airthrey Loch for water sports like sailing and canoeing. Other campus facilities include an art gallery, a post office, a travel agency, a pharmacy, a supermarket, and a small shopping center with a bank. Dining facilities at Stirling are numerous, and there are more than a few pages on the university's web site devoted to their décor and menus.

STUDENT HOUSING AND SERVICES

Stirling houses about 2,300 students on campus in a variety of accommodations. To foster a sense of community and to help them adjust, first-year students living on campus are encouraged to stay in one of the four modern-looking halls of residence overlooking the loch. These are single rooms in suites with shared bathrooms and kitchens. Students report that the accommodations, although not luxurious, "are well kept and have great resources. There is always a porter or someone to complain to if something goes wrong, and it is quickly fixed." Other options include five groups of flats, all with seven single rooms, usually shared between friends. Students can also apply for a space in the 33 five-bedroom "chalets," a very popular option reserved mainly for senior students. These accommodations are highly lauded, especially for their big kitchens and private gardens.

Support services are very comprehensive at Stirling. Students say that "from the union's welfare policy to the university's support network, there are plenty of people to talk to." The campus has its own general medical practitioner and newly built dental center, disability advisor, and chaplaincy. Student support and information services provides academic and personal counseling, and student learning services offers one-on-one study skills workshops through a half-credit course called "Learning Strategies." The university also has an advisor to assist disabled students.

CAMPUS LIFE

What the sleepy town of Stirling lacks in excitement is more than made up for by the campus's rich extracurricular offerings. Stirling University's student association organizes many recreational and international clubs, as well as a student radio station and newspaper. The sports union also sponsors athletic clubs and has a special Clubs Performance program that provides its athletes with coaching, lifestyle counseling, and physical therapy. Students can party in the Robbins Center, the hub of social activity on campus, with four bars and a nightclub, or soak up some culture at the Mac-Robert Arts Center. Its theater hosts student arts programs as well as regular visiting professional groups (including the Royal Shakespeare Company), and its screening room shows everything from blockbusters to student films. With a large student body representing over 70 nationalities on campus, the university has a good mix of cultures, but some international students reported that their U.K. peers were a hard group to infiltrate and that international students tended to stick together.

Students report that although it is small, the city of Stirling offers excellent nightlife. There are a number of live music clubs as well as "the usual nightclub scene." Thursday nights are traditional student nights in the city with most of the clubs and bars offering special prices on admission and discounted drinks promotions.

ADMISSIONS AND FINANCIAL INFO

Students with American high school credentials are expected to have at least two AP tests with scores of 3, or a 4.0 GPA. Apply through UCAS (see page 245).

The university offers some international sports scholarships. Contact the international office for more details.

 CONTACTS

International Office
University of Stirling
Stirling FK9 4LA
Scotland

Phone: 44-1786-467046
Fax: 44-1786-466800
E-mail: international@stir.ac.uk
URL: www.stir.ac.uk

University of Strathclyde

Glasgow, Scotland

AT A GLANCE

One of Scotland's largest universities with strong business and arts programs, the University of Strathclyde offers students a very wide array of facilities on its big-city "Glaswegian" campus.

> **Total Enrollment:** 15,000; 10% international
> **Undergraduate Enrollment:** 11,262
> **Male/Female:** 51/49
> **SAT Scores:** 1300 required
> **Tuition:** $7,000–$13,000 per year depending on the course

CAMPUS AND LOCATION

The University of Strathclyde's history is a varied one. In 1796, John Anderson, a professor at Glasgow University, died and left in his will the funding to start a university open to students regardless of gender or class. His vision was realized, and by the 1890s Anderson's University (renamed the Royal Technical College) had become an important technical and research-based institution. In the late '50s the college merged with the Scottish College of Commerce, was given Royal Charter, and was renamed the University of Strathclyde. In 1993, Strathclyde merged once more with Jordanhill College of Education, Scotland's premier teacher training college, which became the university's Faculty of Education. Today, with 67 buildings on over 500 acres of land, Strathclyde is the third-largest university in Scotland. Its two main campuses, the John Anderson campus and the Jordanhill campus, are located in Glasgow, one of Scotland's largest cities. A major university town, Glasgow offers tons of cultural attractions and many, many pubs. Students also enjoy exploring the beautiful countryside and highlands surrounding Glasgow. For info on arts and entertainment around town, check out **www.glasgow.inyourcity.com**.

ACADEMICS

Strathclyde offers undergraduate degrees across five faculties: Arts and Social Sciences, Education, Engineering, Science, and Strathclyde Business School. Courses are comprised of required and elective classes, discussions, and class projects. The university works on a credit-based modular system. Most modules involve 90 hours of class time, spread out over two 12-week sessions with a revision and mid-sessional examination block in January.

FACILITIES

Strathclyde has invested lots of money in high-tech teaching, and many classrooms are designed with network connections at students' desks. The university is a partner in the Clyde Virtual University, which enables on-line studying, chats, assessments, and access to electronic library resources. There are libraries on each of Strathclyde's two campuses. The Andersonian Library on the John Anderson campus has two branches—the Fleck Chemistry Library and the Law Library. The Jordanhill Library on the Jordanhill campus is the biggest education library in Scotland. Computer labs are available on both campuses.

The John Anderson campus is home to a large sports hall with facilities for all major indoor sports, including squash courts, a weight training area, and a new cardiovascular exercise room with over 50 machines. On the Jordanhill campus, there are two halls used for a variety of indoor games, three gyms, a squash court, a weight training room, a swimming pool, and outdoor playing facilities. East of the city, the university playing field at Stepps features an artificial grass field for hockey, rugby, American football, shinty (a traditional Scottish sport, **www.shinty.com**), and soccer.

STUDENT HOUSING AND SERVICES

The university houses about 1,440 students on its John Anderson campus and another 500 in university residences off campus. All bedrooms in residence halls are equipped with telephones and high-speed internet connections, but students report that rooms are very small. Eighty percent of residences consist of the more popular self-catered flats with a single or shared room and common kitchens. The Jordanhill campus has three additional fully-catered residence halls.

Both campuses have health clinics, and the chaplaincy center in John Street offers services to all faiths and runs the Ark Café. The international office assists foreign students, and the welfare office in the student association offers a student-run, staff-supported enquiry service for all students. Students are also assigned a personal counselor whom they usually meet with two to four times a year to discuss academic issues.

CAMPUS LIFE

The university student union plays a huge role in student life at Strathclyde. It sponsors over 100 student clubs and societies, including a university radio station and newspaper. The student union's Bubble Lounge, one of the biggest bars in Scotland, has live music or DJs every night, and also hosts comedy and film nights. For a comprehensive web site on all aspects of student life, and to listen to the student radio station, visit **www.strathstudents.co.uk.**

The John Anderson campus offers a recreational sports program with a range of classes, fitness testing, and health and lifestyle consultations. The sports union provides competitive and recreational sports for the university community and coordinates about 50 clubs.

Glasgow is a big city with great nightlife and a terrific music scene. (For information on local bands and shows, check out **www. glasgowbands.com.**) Students enjoy hanging out in the many cafés around town, especially around the Gallery of Modern Art.

ADMISSIONS AND FINANCIAL INFO

International students apply through UCAS (see page 245). For details and information on possible scholarship opportunities, contact the international office.

 CONTACTS

University of Strathclyde
International and Graduate Office, Level 4
Graham Hills Building
50 George Street
Glasgow G1 1QE
Scotland

Phone: 44-141-548-2816
Fax: 44-141-552-7493
E-mail: international@mis.strath.ac.uk
URL: www.strath.ac.uk

In order to make the next edition of *Study Away* as comprehensive as possible, we want your feedback. After you've read the book, please visit our web site at **www.collegeabroadguide.com** to tell us what you liked or didn't like about the book or to share your own study abroad experiences.

INDEX

INDEX

PHOTO PERMISSIONS

Grateful acknowledgment is made to the following for permission to reprint photographs:

Page 40. Photograph courtesy of the University of Melbourne.

Page 61. Photograph courtesy of the American University in Bulgaria.

Page 69. Photograph courtesy of Dalhousie University.

Page 91. Photograph courtesy of the University of British Columbia.

Page 102. Photograph courtesy the University of Hong Kong.

Page 114. Photograph courtesy of the American University in Cairo.

Page 130. Photograph by H. Rehling. Copyright © 2003 by the International University of Bremen. Reprinted courtesy of the International University of Bremen.

Page 154. Photograph courtesy of St. George's University.

Page 168. Photograph courtesy of the American University of Rome.

Page 230. Photograph courtesy of Franklin College.

Page 254. Photograph courtesy of British American College London.

Page 291. Photograph courtesy of the University of Edinburgh.

Page 305. Photograph by Jennifer Shields.